When All Else Fails

When All Else Fails

THE ETHICS OF RESISTANCE
TO STATE INJUSTICE

Jason Brennan

PRINCETON UNIVERSITY PRESS

PRINCETON AND OXFORD

Published by Princeton University Press,
41 William Street, Princeton, New Jersey 08540

In the United Kingdom: Princeton University Press,
6 Oxford Street, Woodstock, Oxfordshire OX20 1TR

press.princeton.edu

ISBN 978-0-691-18171-4
LCCN 2018946999

British Library Cataloging-in-Publication Data is available

This book has been composed in Sabon LT Std and Avenir Next

Printed on acid-free paper. ∞

Printed in the United States of America

10 9 8 7 6 5 4 3 2 1

Contents

Acknowledgments

Thanks to Heidi Hurd, John Hasnas, Michael Huemer, Alasdair Cochrane, David Boonin, Alasdair Norcross, Guido Pincione, David Schmidtz, Peter Jaworski, Bas van der Vossen, and Bryan Caplan as well as audiences at the University of Hamburg, the University of Arizona, Sheffield University, the University of North Carolina at Chapel Hill, the University of North Carolina at Greensboro, and the University of Colorado for helpful comments and discussion of the ideas and arguments in this book. Thanks to Rob Tempio, my editor at Princeton University Press, for his continued support as well as his important advice about how best to frame this debate.

This book expands on and contains material previously published in Brennan 2016b and Brennan 2017b.

Preface

DANGEROUS PHILOSOPHY

Western philosophy did not really begin with Socrates, but nevertheless, we tell our students a founding myth. Socrates was a gadfly. He demonstrated that the supposedly wisest people in Athens could not answer what seemed like simple questions about their areas of expertise. The pious could not explain what piety is; the just could not explain what justice is. He showed how much people took for granted and how little they could justify their basic assumptions.

This kind of behavior can be dangerous. The Athenians sure didn't like it; they had him executed. But philosophy is not just dangerous for the philosopher.

Philosophy brings our hidden ideas to the surface and exposes unseen contradictions. What we think is obvious is not so obvious on reflection. Philosophical inquiry often shows that our core beliefs are a jumbled mess.

We sometimes make dangerous mistakes when we try to clean up that mess. Some countries today still suffer the legacy of philosophers' past errors.

But at the same time, we do not make progress without challenging and in many cases changing our moral ideas. In general, people live far better and in far more just societies today than a thousand years ago. I don't want to give philosophers all or even most of the credit for that. But philosophers deserve some credit. It matters that we now see government agents as servants appointed by the people rather than as lords appointed by the gods.

It matters that we see people everywhere as part of the same moral community rather than holding, as most early people did, that the "barbarians" outside our borders also fall outside our moral concerns. It matters that we recognize that government leaders and civilians are fundamentally morally equal; there is not one set of rights for the high and a different set for the low.

Philosophy often deals with dangerous subjects and questions: Might belief in divine beings be a mistake? When do humans acquire a right to life? Which rights do we have, how strong are those rights, and when, if ever, may governments or others override them? What are the principles governing war? What makes sexual assault, stealing, or killing wrong? What makes something a moral patient—that is, a thing to which obligations are owed? What makes something a moral agent—that is, a thing that possesses moral obligations? What kind of value does human, animal, or plant life have? When, if ever, is violence permitted or justified?

These are difficult questions. They are difficult in part because most of us have conflicting beliefs and intuitions about these questions. Most people's answers to those questions have implications that they are not prepared to endorse.

For instance, bioethicist Peter Singer asks readers to consider why they believe human beings have rights that, say, cows lack. Most will say something such as, "Well, human beings have free will and cows don't," or "People have sufficiently high intelligence to have rights but cows don't." Singer then responds by saying if that's really the explanation, it suggests that we may feel free to perform medical experiments on or even eat the severely mentally disabled; after all, they lack the special features that you claim imbue people with rights. This of course causes many readers great discomfort. But that kind of discomfort is necessary for us to answer questions about where rights come from and what has them.

This book argues for a rather simple but possibly dangerous idea: you possess the same right of self-defense, and the same right to defend others, against *government agents* as you do against *civilians*. The moral principles governing self-defense against civilians and government agents, even agents who act by virtue of their appointed status and within the law, are the same. The main way I will argue for this position is to show that the reasons to think otherwise are unsound.

This book has straightforwardly dangerous implications. If I am right, this means that when a police officer uses excessive violence against you or tries to arrest you for a crime that should not be a crime, you may defend yourself. It means that agents working within government may sabotage their colleagues or superiors who act unjustly. It means that you may lie to government agents who would use your information in unjust ways.

We need to be cautious here.

This is a book about self-defense and the defense of others. You engage in self-defense against the bully when you fight back as he pushes you. You defend someone else against the would-be mugger when you stop him as he tries to rob his victim. If, on the other hand, you beat up the bully or mugger a year later when they're harming no one, you aren't defending yourself or anyone else. You're exacting revenge or inflicting private punishment. That's not what this book is about. Self-defense and vigilante justice are two different things.

In recent years, you may have watched recorded videos of police officers using excessive force against civilians. In some of those cases, yes, I am arguing that bystanders had the right to use violence, even deadly violence, to stop the police from brutalizing or killing those civilians. But if you take it on yourself to attack those police now, after the fact, you are not defending anyone. You're exacting revenge or inflicting private punishment. That's not what this book defends.

Further, don't confuse self-defense with revolution or violent social change. The principles that I discuss in this book concern in what ways we may defend ourselves or others from immediate threats of injustice. But I am not arguing that we should use violence, subterfuge, or deceit to change the form of government, who rules, what the laws are, or how the laws are enforced.

This is a book of philosophy, not a manual for self-defense. I recommend that you be extremely cautious in applying the ideas of this book. First, I might be wrong. I don't think I am, but I may well be. Second, even if I'm right, in the heat of the moment, it's often hard to apply moral principles correctly, and you may make mistakes. Third, note that while I am arguing that certain forms of defensive action are permissible, the state is almost certainly not going to agree. In, for example, the Rodney King beating, I think it would have been *morally* permissible for a bystander to intervene. But any such bystander should know that the police may have reacted violently to such intervention, and whoever intervened may be charged with a crime or even killed. Sometimes what's morally permissible is also imprudent.

Part of philosophy's job is to critically examine our most basic assumptions and see if these beliefs withstand scrutiny. Doing so is almost guaranteed to offend.

Sometimes what seemed like merely academic discussions became politically salient. In the latter half of the twentieth century, philosophers debated whether torture was always wrong, or whether it might be permissible or at least excusable to extract information from terrorists in "ticking time bomb" cases. Then the United States declared a "War on Terror," and suddenly these discussions were no longer academic.

Similarly, back in 1978, philosopher Philippa Foot introduced the "Trolley Problem." Foot asks us, if a runaway train were about to crush five people, but you could pull a switch to direct it onto a track where it will only kill one, should you—assuming you have no other options— pull the switch? Most people say yes. She then asks us to imagine the same scenario, except this time you can stop the train by pushing a fat man onto the track. Is that permissible? Most people say no. The puzzle is what makes the cases different. Trolley-ology—philosophy examining thousands of variations on cases like these—seemed pointless to many, but now, with the self-driving automobiles, the question is practical, not hypothetical. We need to program these cars to make the right decisions when they encounter problems like these.

This book was inspired by real-life events. It concerns real-life situations. But I should be clear that I have no ill will toward government agents in general. I believe we should honor the good that others do and hold them accountable for their wrongs. I say this in the spirit of equality. We are fundamentally on par from a moral point of view. This book is an attempt to understand what it means to take that moral parity seriously.

When All Else Fails

CHAPTER 1

Resistance

THE FOURTH OPTION

You see the police pull over a black man driving a silver Hyundai.[1] The police explain to the man—let's call him Richard—that only moments ago, he went slightly past the white line at a stoplight before he stopped and took a right turn. (His blinkers were on.) The police demand that Richard step out of the car. He does so quietly and calmly. As he steps out, one officer immediately flips Richard around, bends his arm, and slams Richard against the Hyundai. He then flips Richard around again, and starts punching him in the face and kicking him in the groin. As Richard screams and puts his arms up to protect himself, the other officer joins in. Soon they have Richard prone on the ground, but continue to punch, hammer, and kick him, and smash his face against the ground. All the while—as Richard simply tries to hold his arms up to protect his face—they yell, "Stop resisting!" Even when Richard is completely subdued, lying prostrate with his hands behind his back, with two large officers pinning him down, one officer continues to punch him in the back of the skull.

For all you know, they are going to kill, maim, or severely injure him. He's done nothing to warrant that. A thought occurs to you: you're armed. You could intervene, perhaps saving Richard's life.

May you do so? This book defends a controversial answer: yes, in this case, the police are rightful targets of defensive violence. You would be justified in attacking the officers to save Richard.

EXIT, VOICE, AND LOYALTY

In the real world, almost every day, the people who hold power in democratic societies—including presidents, bureaucrats, judges, police officers, Central Intelligence Agency (CIA) agents, and even democratic voters—use their power in deeply unjust and irresponsible ways. Thus, one pressing question for political philosophy is what ordinary citizens are licensed to do in the face of injustice.

In the famous book *Exit, Voice, and Loyalty*, political economist Albert Hirschman analyzed three major ways that a firm's customers or an organization's members might react to bad behavior on the part of the firm or organization.[2] They might "exit," meaning that customers might stop buying their products or members of the organization (such as employees) might leave. They might exercise "voice," meaning that they might complain to people in the organization itself, such as people who hold power over the organization, or the public at large. Finally, they might be *loyal*—that is, they might have a tendency to stick with the firm or organization despite their flaws. Hirschman does not say that loyalty is always an alternative to voice or exit. Instead, loyal behavior can augment one's voice or threat of exit.

Many philosophers and laypeople seem to believe that when we react to political oppression and injustice, our options are limited to voice, exit, or loyalty. Some think that we have obligations to participate in politics, protest, engage in political campaigns, and push for social change through political channels.[3] Others think that such actions are merely praiseworthy. Most think that we have the option of keeping quiet or emigrating to another country. In general, they tend to assume or conclude that when a government issues an unjust command, behaves unjustly, or passes an unjust law, we may only comply, complain, or quit. Usually, we should obey that law, or if we break the law in protest, we should be prepared to bear the consequences of doing so, including accepting punishment.[4] They typically tend to agree that we may not fight back against government agents, especially agents of a democratic regime.

Consider the question of defensive assassination or defensive killing. Andrew Altman and Christopher Wellman say, "Surely, it would have been permissible for somebody to assassinate [Joseph] Stalin in the 1930s."[5] But if so, is it not also permissible to take similar action against a government official if it is the only way to stop them from harming the innocent? If you may assassinate Adolf Hitler to stop him from invading Poland, are you also permitted to do the same to a president in order to stop him from invading the Philippines, or ordering the genocidal slaughter and forced relocation of an ethnic group? If you may kill a Gestapo agent to stop him from murdering innocent people, may you do the same to a police officer who uses excessive violence?

As I noted, philosophers and laypeople often assume or argue not. They assume or argue that in liberal democracies, only nonviolent resistance to state injustice is permissible. They assume that we must defer to democratic government agents, even when these agents act in deeply unjust, harmful, and destructive ways.

This view is puzzling. The prevailing view is that when it comes to government agents, defensive violence, deception, destruction, and subterfuge are governed by different moral principles from those that govern defensive violence and subterfuge in other contexts. This presupposes that it makes a difference to the permissibility of lying to, deceiving, sabotaging, or killing an aggressor in self-defense or the defense of others that the aggressor is wearing a uniform, holds an office, or was appointed by someone who was in turn elected by my neighbors. According to the prevailing view, my neighbors can eliminate my right of self-defense or the defense of others by granting someone an office.[6] This is especially puzzling because almost everyone today recognizes that the law and justice are not the same thing; laws can be deeply unjust.

Instead of exit, voice, or loyalty, this book defends the fourth option: resistance.[7] I'm using "resistance" to cover a wide range of behaviors. It includes passive behaviors such as noncompliance—that is, strategically breaking the law or ignoring the state's commands whenever you can get away with it. It also includes more active forms of resistance, such as blocking police cars, damaging or destroying government property, deceiving and lying to government agents, or combating government agents. My view is that such forms of resistance are often justified, even in response to injustice within modern democratic nation-states, most of which have relatively just governments overall.

GOVERNMENTS ARE MAGIC: THE SPECIAL IMMUNITY THESIS

The standard view, which almost everyone of every ideology seems to accept, is that government agents are surrounded by a kind of magic moral force field. They enjoy a special or privileged status when they commit unjust actions. The standard view holds both that government agents have a special permission to perform unjust actions—actions that we would judge evil and impermissible were a nongovernment agent to perform them—and that these agents enjoy a special right against being *stopped* when they commit injustice. Government agents somehow *may* perform unjust acts, and we're supposed to stand by and *let them.*

Maybe "let them" is a bit strong. Most people believe we may *complain* when government agents act badly. We may demand that *other* government agents punish their colleagues for their colleagues' bad behavior. Some philosophers go further: they think that when government acts badly, we are morally obligated to protest, write letters to newspaper editors and senators, and vote for better candidates.[8] But, they think, we're not supposed to *stop* injustice ourselves.

We don't think that way about private injustice. If an attacker tries to harm you, no one would say that you have no right to fight back. You aren't required to lie down and take it, and then hope the police will later capture the attacker and bring them to justice.

Some political philosophers and laypeople would scoff. They claim that they have a far more constrained and reasonable version of the "government agents are magic" view. They deny that all governments, government agents, or political actors enjoy special permission to perform unjust actions. They deny that we must stand back and let government actors behave unjustly. Rather, they say, "In our modest view, only *democratic* governments, agents, and actors are surrounded by a magic moral force field that both removes their normal moral obligations and at the same time requires the rest of us to *let* them act unjustly. Of course, *nondemocratic* governments and their agents enjoy no such privilege."

To illustrate what I mean by the "government agents are magic" view, consider the following four thought experiments or examples:

A. Shooter in the Park

A masked man emerges from a black van holding a rifle. He starts shooting at children in a public park. Ann, a bystander, has a gun. She kills him before he kills any innocent children.

B. Drunk Partygoer

Rodney has too much to drink at a party. He runs around the house with a tiki torch, loudly yelling, "Look, everyone, I'm the Human Torch!" Four partygoers chase him outside to stop him from accidentally starting a fire. In their anger, they knock him down. They continuously kick his face and stomach, and beat him with bats and sticks. Ann sees that Rodney is subdued, and sees that the men beating him are carrying pistols, though they aren't using them. She pulls out her gun and yells for them to stop, but they ignore her. Finally, she pulls out her own weapon and shoots one of them in order to stop the beating as well as possibly save Rodney's life.

C. Health Nut

Health guru John sincerely believes that caffeine is unhealthy, causes laziness, and induces people to use hard drugs. John announces that in order to protect his neighbors and promote the social good, he and his followers will capture coffee drinkers, confiscate their belongings, and imprison them in John's filthy basement for years. Ann, who is too poor to move away from town, loves coffee. She secretly drinks it in the morning in her kitchen. One day, a follower of John breaks into her house and attempts to capture her. She struggles to defend herself, and in the process, kills him.

D. Terrorist

Cobra Commander, leader of the terrorist organization COBRA, uses a combination of bribes, subterfuge, and threats to get the leaders of the United States to do his bidding. He then gets the US military to perform an unjust invasion of another country. Ann, who is a private security guard, realizes that the individual she's protecting is secretly Cobra Commander and discovers his plot. Right before Cobra Commander issues an order that will kill hundreds of innocent civilians, she shoots him in the back of the head.

Normally it is wrong to hurt or kill other people. But in these examples, Ann may kill the wrongdoers because doing so is the most effective means to protect herself or others from suffering severe harm or injustice. If Ann had some sufficiently effective nonviolent means of protecting herself or others, perhaps she would be obligated to use those means instead. Since she doesn't, though, she's permitted to use violence to stop others from committing severe injustices. She's not required to *allow* the wrongdoers to commit their atrocities. She's not required to stand back and let them commit evil.

I expect most people believe it's permissible for Ann to kill the wrongdoers in these four cases. Probably only radical pacifists would say that killing is wrong.[9]

Now consider four new cases (A'–D') that seem analogous to the first four (A–D). In these new cases, the only obvious major difference is that the wrongdoer is the agent, acting ex officio, of a government. (If you wish, go ahead and assume that the wrongdoer is the agent of a *democratic* government.) Note that the first three cases below are based loosely on variations of real-life news stories.

A'. Minivan Shooter

Ann witnesses a police officer stop a minivan with a female driver and three children in the back. Ann sees that the driver has nothing in her hands and her hands are on the steering wheel. The police officer emerges from his car and starts shooting at the van's windows. Ann has a gun. She fires at the police officer before he shoots any of the children.[10]

B'. Drunk Driver

Rodney, intoxicated after a night spent drinking, starts speeding on the highway. The cops try to pull him over. He ignores them, and then a high-speed chase ensues. When the cops finally pull him over, they do not merely yank him out of the car and arrest him. Rather, even after he is subdued and lying prostrate on the ground, they take turns clubbing him with their batons. Ann witnesses the beating and yells for them to stop. The police ignore her. Finally, she pulls out her own weapon and shoots one of them in order to stop the beating as well as possibly save Rodney's life.[11]

C'. War on Drugs

Town leaders decide to make marijuana illegal, even though there is overwhelming evidence that marijuana is in every respect less harmful than alcohol—a drug that is legal for any adult to consume.[12] Ann has a pot stash in her house. One night, the police raid Ann's house in a no-knock raid. She recognizes that they are police officers.

She also knows that if they capture her, she will be imprisoned for a long time. Her government issues overly punitive sentences for drug possession and is unresponsive to citizens' demands to overturn the law. Ann resists arrest and escapes.[13]

D'. Hawk

Ann, a secret service agent, happens to be in the situation room when she hears the president order the unjust invasion of another country. Right before the president issues an order that—as the generals and other experts in the room make clear—will kill hundreds of innocent civilians, she knocks him out.

People tend to judge these four new cases differently from the first set. They think intervening in self-defense or the defense others is wrongful in (at least some of) A'–D', even though it was permissible in A–D. At least at first glance, however, A–D seems analogous to A'–D', except that the wrongdoers are private civilians in A–D but are government agents acting ex officio in A'–D'.

Most people would endorse similarly differing judgments in other kinds of cases. I may lie to the Mafia to stop it from hurting innocent people. But I may not lie to the Canadian voters for the same end. I may hack into and sabotage the Mafia's computers, or sabotage its finances (if I'm in an accounting firm), to stop it from hurting innocent people. Yet I may not do these things to stop the German government from hurting innocent people. I may destroy the Mafia's gun stash to stop it from hurting the innocent. But I may not destroy the British Army's weapons even as it's about to start an unjust war.

Now without filling in all the details, one might think these different cases are not morally analogous. Maybe if we think carefully, we'll see that these cases are not much alike. Perhaps A–D is not really similar to A'–D'. So over the course of the book, we'll check to see if there are any important disanalogies.

Still, at first glance, there seem to be plenty of real-life examples in which governments, including democratic ones, commit horrifically unjust actions. If a private agent tried to perform these same actions, we would think it permissible to stop them, using deception, sabotage, or violence if need be. Yet for various reasons, people think that when governments and their agents perform these actions, we're supposed to *let* them do it. They allow that we may, or perhaps demand that we must, complain afterward, but they say we must not *stop* them ourselves.

Thus, many people subscribe to what I call the *special immunity thesis*. The special immunity thesis holds that there is a special burden to justify interfering with, trying to stop, or fighting back against government agents who, acting ex officio, commit injustice:

The Special Immunity Thesis

Government agents—or at least the agents of democratic governments—enjoy a special immunity against being deceived, lied to, sabotaged, attacked, or killed in self-defense or the defense of others. Government property enjoys a special immunity against being damaged, sabotaged, or destroyed. The set of conditions under which it is permissible, in self-defense or the defense of others, to deceive, lie to, sabotage, or use force against a government agent (acting ex officio), or destroy government property, is much more stringent as well as tightly constrained than the set of conditions under which it is permissible to deceive, lie to, sabotage, attack, or kill a private civilian, or destroy private property.

In contrast, I reject the special immunity thesis in favor of the *moral parity thesis*:

The Moral Parity Thesis

The conditions under which a person may, in self-defense or the defense of others, deceive, lie to, sabotage, attack, or kill a fellow civilian, or destroy private property, are also conditions under which a civilian may do the same to a government agent (acting ex officio) or government property.

The moral parity thesis holds that justifying self-defense or the defense of others against government agents is on par with justifying self-defense or the defense of others against civilians.

IN DEFENSE OF MORAL PARITY

The main conclusions of this book are simple:

- *The special immunity thesis is false.*
- *The morality parity thesis is true.*

I defend the view that government officials (including the officials of democratic governments, acting ex officio) do not enjoy a special moral status that immunizes them from defensive actions. When government officials commit injustices of *any* sort, it is morally permissible for us, as private individuals, to treat them the same way we would treat private individuals committing those same injustices. Whatever we may do to private individuals, we may do to government officials. We may respond to governmental injustice however we may respond to private injustice. Government agents are due no greater moral deference when they act unjustly than private agents are due.

The moral parity thesis holds that democratic government agents, property, and agencies are as much legitimate targets of defensive deception, sabotage, or violence as civilians are. The principles explaining how we may use defensive violence and subterfuge against civilians, and the principles explaining how we may use defensive violence and subterfuge against government agents, are one and the same. Government agents (including citizens when they vote) who commit injustice are on par with civilians who commit the same injustices.

To some, this may not sound like a controversial thesis. If, however, we combine the moral parity thesis with commonsense moral thinking about defensive lying, sabotage, and violence, plus a frank and realistic appraisal of how governments often behave, we may have to grapple with or accept a number of controversial and unsettling claims. For example:

1. It may be permissible to assassinate presidents, representatives, generals, and others to stop them from waging unjust wars, even if those wars enjoy widespread popular support and are ratified through legal means. It is also permissible to kill them to stop them from issuing certain unjust orders even if the war they are fighting is, overall, justified.

2. It may be permissible to use force to resist a law enforcement official trying to arrest you when you have broken a bad or unjust law, such as laws criminalizing marijuana or homosexual sex.[14]

3. If you are imprisoned for doing something that should not be a crime (e.g., you harbor an escaped slave in 1850s'

America or you have consensual homosexual sex in 1940s' England), you may permissibly try to break free.

4. Political candidates may sometimes lie to ignorant, irrational, misinformed, or malicious voters in order to stop them from getting their way.

5. Corporations, and private individuals or businesses, may lie about their compliance with wrongful or punitive regulations.

6. A person may join the military or a government bureaucracy in order to sabotage some of its operations from within.

7. You may engage in tax evasion to avoid unjust taxes.

8. Soldiers may ignore unjust orders, and in some cases, subdue or fight back against the officers who issue them. They may also in certain cases kill their fellow soldiers who try to follow those unjust orders.

9. You may use force against a police officer to stop excessive violence.

10. It can be permissible to find, steal, and publicize certain state secrets, such as some, if not all, the secrets Julian Assange, Edward Snowden, or Chelsea Manning revealed.

11. US Supreme Court (or equivalent) justices may lie about what the written or unwritten Constitution allows or forbids. They may refuse to enforce or apply unjust laws.

And so on.

These seemingly radical conclusions follow from commonsense moral principles plus the moral parity thesis.

While lying, sabotaging, hurting, destroying, and killing are usually wrong, commonsense holds that we may do these things, either in self-defense or the defense of others, under the right circumstances. This book's conclusions seem radical only because we tend to assume that government agents are to be held to a *lower* moral standard than we hold civilians and that government agents enjoy a special immunity against defensive action. These assumptions are unfounded. Philosophers have spent twenty-five hundred years trying to justify these assumptions, but their arguments fail.

To be more precise, the moral parity thesis simply says that government agents and private wrongdoers may be treated the same. On its own, it does not tell us what we may or may not do to stop wrongdoers. It only says that government wrongdoers have no special protection against interference or violence in virtue of being government agents. To settle just how we may treat government wrongdoers, we need to answer two other questions— one moral, and the other empirical:

- *Moral Question: Just what are the conditions under which it would be permissible for a private civilian (or group) to lie, deceive, sabotage, destroy, attack, or kill in self-defense or the defense of others?*
- *Empirical Question: Just how often do those conditions obtain?*

Strictly speaking, in this book I could remain neutral on these two questions. Almost all my arguments are dedicated to defending the moral parity thesis and exploring some of its implications. That said, I'll assume and discuss what I regard as relatively uncontroversial as well as commonsense answers to the moral question. In later chapters, I'll take note of how people disagree on some of the finer details of the moral question, but I'll remain mostly neutral on these intramural debates.

DEFENSIVE ACTION VERSUS CIVIL DISOBEDIENCE

This book concerns a class of actions I will call "defensive actions." I use terms like defensive actions or "defensive resistance" to refer broadly to acts of lying, cheating, stealing, sabotaging, destroying, attacking, and killing in self-defense or the defense of others. I'll use "defensive force" or "defensive violence" to refer more specifically to destroying, attacking, and killing in self-defense or the defensive of others. (So defensive violence is a type of defensive action, but not all defensive actions are also forms of defensive violence.) My main thesis is that government agents do not enjoy a special immunity against defensive actions.

This book is not about *civil disobedience,* at least not in the specialized way that philosophers and legal theorists tend to use that term. As the philosopher Kimberly Brownlee elaborates, when a person engages in civil disobedience, that "person typically has both forward-looking and backward-looking aims. She seeks not only to convey her disavowal and condemnation of a certain law or policy, but also to draw public attention to this particular issue and thereby to instigate a change in law or policy."[15] Civil disobedience is a public act. The disobedient citizen publicly and openly breaks some law or regulation with the goal of drawing attention to her disobedience. She hopes that her disobedience will induce the public to support her cause. Disobedient citizens often accept punishment, not necessarily because they think punishment is warranted, but instead because they believe accepting punishment will demonstrate their sincere commitment or selflessness, or it will shame the public into changing. Ultimately, the goal of civil disobedience is to change various laws, regulations, or social practices, or replace government leaders, to change the form of government or win the right to secede. In short, civil disobedience is a particular method for inducing social and political change.

In this book, I am not concerned with the morality or strategic effectiveness of civil disobedience so defined. This is a book about self-defense and the defense of others against particular acts of injustice rather than about inducing social change. To illustrate this, consider the differences between these two examples:

The Smoke-In

The National Organization for the Reform of Marijuana Laws, Marijuana Policy Project, Students for Sensible Drug Policy, and other marijuana legalization advocates organize a national "smoke-in" day. A million citizens agree to converge on the National Mall in Washington, DC, to smoke pot in public. Participants agree to hold signs indicating what kinds of jobs or lifestyles they have in order to make it clear that many different kinds of people, including high-status and responsible citizens, use pot. The organizers ensure the event generates massive press coverage. Participants agree not to resist arrest. Certain civil rights organizations agree to provide legal counsel for anyone arrested.

Just Say No to False Arrest

Ann is walking down the street when a cop with a K9 stops her. The dog indicates it smells drugs in her possession. In fact, Ann has a few joints in her pocket, which she plans to smoke at home. The cop tries to arrest her. Ann pepper sprays the cop and dog, and flees.

The first example is a case of civil disobedience. The second is a case of defensive action. (If you want, call it "uncivil disobedience.") In the first instance, the participants are trying to change the law. In the second, Ann is simply defending herself from government injustice. She isn't trying to change the marijuana laws; she's trying to defend herself.

WHEN ALL ELSE FAILS: THE MORALITY OF CAUTION

Violence, deception, destruction, and sabotage might not always be last resorts, but they are rarely first resorts. Well-functioning societies create nonviolent means to resolve disputes and disagreements. Decent people try to resolve disagreements though nonviolent means when possible. There are good reasons to minimize violence, not just in general, but even in response to violence from others. Sometimes violence is called for, but it's not something to celebrate.

It's usually better (and sometimes obligatory) that we resolve our disputes and disagreements peacefully. Sometimes the best response to injustice is even to suck it up and live with it, or turn the other cheek. When nonviolent forms of mediation or conflict resolution are available, we should generally use them, and we sometimes should accept incorrectly decided outcomes. People frequently disagree about fundamental principles of justice and what the relevant facts are. Given that problem, often what makes a law good isn't so much that it tracks justice perfectly but rather that it provides a workable compromise everyone can live with.

All this applies to interpersonal conflicts. Suppose you crash your car into mine. Suppose you really owe me $3,000 in damages. But suppose both our insurance companies, plus an impartial mediator, mistakenly yet in good faith settle on $2,700. I should let it go rather than hack your bank account for the other $300.

Similarly, I will accept that these same standards apply to conflicts with the state when it acts badly. The point of this book is not to advocate we burn down the capital or start lynching cops. Instead, it's much more modest: we should feel free to treat the state and its agents the way we treat each other. It's just that once we accept this claim—that political actors do not enjoy special immunity—then resistance becomes a viable fourth option in responding to their misbehavior.

Here I introduce some distinctions to help clarify how we should think about these issues. Consider the difference between what we might call *strategic* versus *principled nonviolence*. The doctrine of strategic nonviolence, the one that Martin Luther King Jr. most likely advocated, holds that people who are trying to produce social change should avoid violence because peaceful methods are more likely to succeed.[16] King thought nonviolence was more likely to elicit sympathetic responses from others. For instance, if protesters refuse to fight back when the police attack them, people watching at home might view the protesters as especially noble and would then be likely to support the cause. If the protesters fought back, TV viewers may conclude the protesters are getting what they deserve. Viewers would be more likely to side with the state or police. Moreover, those who defend strategic nonviolence often worry that if citizens fight back against injustice, the state or its agents will *retaliate* by committing even greater injustices.

While strategic nonviolence holds that nonviolence "works" better, what we might call principled nonviolence maintains that violence is wrong, period, regardless of how well it "works." Pacifist Anabaptists, for example, refused to fight back against oppression, not because they believed their pacifism would shame their oppressors into change, but because they thought defensive violence was wrong in itself, period. They took Christ's injunction to turn the other cheek to mean that they were required to, well, turn the other cheek.

Again, this book is about using defensive violence, deception, and sabotage to stop individual acts of injustice. I am not much concerned with offering a theory of social change—that is, a theory of how best to change laws, institutions, or prevailing social norms.[17]

That said, when we later examine various objections to defensive violence, deception, and sabotage, or consider the various arguments people might offer in favor of the special immunity thesis, we should be careful to consider whether these assertions invoke strategic or principled concerns. If someone says, "You shouldn't fight back against a cop trying to arrest you for possessing marijuana because then people will lose sympathy for the marijuana decriminalization movement," that person appears to invoke a strategic argument for nonviolence. If the person says, "You shouldn't fight back against a cop trying to arrest you for possessing marijuana because cops have a right to be obeyed," that person invokes a principled objection to resistance.

Here's another important distinction. Consider case A' again:

A'. Minivan Shooter

Ann witnesses a police officer stop a minivan with a female driver and three children in the back. Ann sees that the driver has nothing in her hands and her hands are on the steering wheel. The police officer emerges from his car and starts shooting at the van's windows. Ann has a gun. She fires at the police officer before he shoots any of the children.

Now consider two different objections (among many) people might produce against Ann shooting the police officer:

- *Moral Authority: While it's wrong for the police officer to shoot at the children, Ann has a duty to obey and defer to the police. Even if she knows for certain that what he's doing is wrong, she must allow him to do it rather than stop him. She may/must instead report him to his superior officer.*
- *Epistemic Uncertainty: It's strange and unusual for police officers to attempt to murder innocent people. Though it seems like that's what the police officer is doing, Ann should give the officer the benefit of the doubt and presume that he has some unknown but good reason to do what he's doing. She should not kill him—at least not until she gathers more information.*

These objections raise two different kinds of reasons against Ann shooting the cop.

The first is a principled moral objection, which holds that it's just wrong, period, for Ann to shoot the cop. Ann knows what the cop is doing is wrong, but she has a duty to let him act wrongly. Just as subjects must obey their king even if he issues an unjust command, Ann must defer to the cop.

The second is (or could be interpreted as) another kind of strategic objection. It doesn't say strictly speaking that shooting the officer is wrong. Rather, it's offering advice about how a person in Ann's situation ought to think. It allows that her intervention might indeed be permissible. But it advises Ann to be suspicious and self-critical when she reaches that conclusion. The idea is that it's unusual for someone like Ann to be in a situation where it's right to shoot a law enforcement official. She should be cautious in reaching the judgment that defensive action is called for. She should presume that the officer has some unknown justification for his behavior.

In chapter 4, we'll explore further worries about epistemic uncertainty and moral caution. I'll agree that actors who are considering lying, cheating, stealing, engaging in sabotage or violence, or using violence should be cautious about what they think they know. Nevertheless, I'll show that all this is compatible with the moral parity thesis.

As we'll see in chapter 2 when we review the common-sense doctrine of defensive action, it is not necessary that the defender eliminate uncertainty in order to be justified in using defensive action. To use defensive violence, one should justifiably believe that doing so is necessary to defend oneself or others. But to be justified doesn't require that one be *certain*. So, for instance, suppose tonight as I'm sleeping, plainclothes police officers mistakenly invade my house in a no-knock raid. In the heat of the moment, I'm likely to be unsure of whether the invaders are police officers or robbers. It would, I'll argue, be justifiable for me to shoot first and ask questions later. *All* the potential downsides and risks should fall on the police, and *they*, not my family and I, should bear all the risks from uncertainty about what's happening.

THINGS I DON'T ASSUME AND THAT DON'T MATTER FOR THIS DEBATE

Let's clear up some possible misconceptions up front.

I am not arguing for anarchism. Following the philosopher Gregory Kavka, I understand a *government* to be the subset of a society that claims a monopoly on the legitimate use of coercion, and has coercive power sufficient (more or less) to maintain that monopoly.[18] Anarchists generally believe that governments are unjust. Or more weakly, they believe nongovernmental mechanisms for protecting rights and property, or maintaining public goods, are all things considered superior to governmental mechanisms.[19] Whether anarchist alternatives to government are feasible is, I think, a far more interesting question than most people realize, but this book takes no stance on these issues.[20]

As I will elaborate at greater length in chapter 3, I can assume (for the sake of argument) that we ought to have governments rather than not, and furthermore, that the governments in question generally are legitimate, and may permissibly create and enforce rules. As I'll show in chapter 3, I could even grant for the sake of argument that governments have permission to create and enforce bad, unjust, or downright evil rules. At no point will I argue for *revolution*—that is, overthrowing any governments, and replacing them with other forms of government or anarchist alternatives. Nevertheless, even with those assumptions and constraints, the main thesis of this book goes through.

I also do not argue for, and my argument does not assume, libertarianism or classical liberalism. Libertarians and classical liberals are generally skeptical of the state and state authority.[21] They do not view the state or its agents as majestic. They think the slogan "government is simply the name we give to the things we choose to do together" is utterly ridiculous.[22] For that reason, they are statistically more likely than others to accept the conclusions of this book. Yet the argument I make here is compatible with a wide range of background political philosophies, including both left and right anarchism, left liberalism, progressivism, US conservatism, Burkean conservatism, Rawlsianism, and classical liberalism.[23]

This book presumes no particular background moral theory. I will argue on the basis of widely shared intuitions and moral principles, but I will not try to ground these principles on any particular philosophical theory of morality. My reasoning is compatible with various forms of consequentialism, Kantianism, natural law theory, and other moral theories. Of course, not everything I say is compatible with every view. I'll assert later that justice and morality are not merely decided by legal or democratic fiat (except perhaps in narrow cases), and so my view is incompatible with those that say the opposite.

I'm not being evasive here. Rather, it's important to recognize what's at stake in an argument and what isn't. Most moral theories and theories of justice are highly abstract. Asking what some grand moral theory like Kantianism implies about the right of self-defense is a bit like asking what Albert Einstein's field equations say about the path of a falling feather.[24] Einstein's field equations describe the general ordering of space and time. They are highly abstract and devoid of specific empirical information. The equations are consistent with worlds radically different from ours, such as Kurt Gödel's universe.[25] By themselves, the field equations tell us little about the physics of a falling feather. To understand the falling feather, we use intermediary or midlevel physical laws and models, and the laws and models we'd use are ultimately compatible with Newtonian or relativistic physics.

I think something similar holds true for most—and the most interesting—questions in political philosophy and ethics. To answer these questions, we need to make use of intermediary or midlevel moral principles, but these principles are compatible with a wide range of background moral theories. To answer the questions in this book, we don't need to take a stance on whether Kantianism is correct, any more than to design a jet engine well, we need to take a stance on whether string theory is correct.

WHY IT MATTERS TODAY

Political philosophy aspires to a kind of timelessness. This book does too. I believe that the basic principles I defend here were true two thousand years ago and will be true two thousand years in the future.

That said, current events give this topic special interest. Every day we see videos of or read stories about police beating unarmed people, burning toddlers, or choking nonviolent criminals to death.[26] US police killed about a thousand people in 2015, and approximately another thousand in 2016.[27]

Unfortunately, there do not seem to be good data on the number of police-caused deaths over time. While it's clear that the US police are more militarized and aggressive overall now than they were forty years ago, it's unclear whether they really are more violent or abusive, or whether ubiquitous cell phone cameras and social media just mean that we're more aware of their behavior.[28]

Right now the US government, at both the federal and local levels, suffers from a crisis of perceived illegitimacy.

President Donald Trump, even more than his far-from-innocent predecessors, seems happy to ignore constitutional constraints.

The US federal government tries hard to exempt itself from due process. It regularly spies on citizens and gives itself permission to assassinate them.[29] It tortures foreigners and launches wave after wave of unjust wars. Democracy seems impotent to fix the problem. Agencies are largely autonomous, and these kinds of activities continue regardless of whom we vote into power.

In a recent *CounterPunch* article defending the Black Panthers, Thandisizwe Chimurenga asks us to "imagine that, instead of bystanders filming CHP Officer Daniel Andrew mercilessly beating a helpless Marlene Pinnock by the side of the I-10 freeway last August, a handful of those bystanders had trained their weapons on Andrew, demanded he cease and desist, handcuffed him and waited until a commander from the CHP arrived on the scene."[30] This is precisely the kind of problem I have in mind. I doubt handcuffing Andrew would have worked; I suspect the cops would have sent a SWAT team to kill anyone who intervened. Still, I agree with Chimurenga that, if the facts are as he states them, some form of violent intervention would be morally permissible, though probably imprudent.

On YouTube, you can watch police violently beat Noel Aguilar, whom the police claimed had a gun and was resisting arrest. At one point, while two officers crush Aguilar beneath their knees, an officer draws his pistol and attempts to shoot Aguilar. The officer misses and hits his partner. Both officers then shoot Aguilar multiple times.[31]

In another video, police officer Patrick Feaster pursues Andrew Thomas, who had run a red light. Thomas eventually crashes and flips his car, which ejects and kills his wife. Feaster's own dash cam video shows Thomas crawling out of his window. Almost as soon as Thomas emerges from the car, his hands clearly free of any weapons, Feaster shoots Thomas in the neck.[32]

People dispute what the facts are. But as I'll argue in future chapters, in at least some cases like these, it would be justifiable for the onlookers to put down their camera phones and instead forcefully intervene to stop the police from using excessive as well as reckless force, or in some extreme cases, stop the officers from *executing* their victims.

All this holds true even in reasonably just democratic states. Compared to nondemocratic alternatives, democratic states do a decent job defending civil rights.[33] Their agents tend to behave better than agents who work in other forms of government. Democracies provide legal, peaceful avenues to stop leaders from committing injustices.

That said, there are realistic circumstances in which democratic leaders and agents do deeply unjust things that go far beyond anything that could plausibly be seen as their authoritative scope of power. Consider essayist Alfred Jay Nock's moral indictment of the United States on the eve of World War II:

> In order to keep down the great American sin of self-righteousness, every public presentation ought to draw the deadly parallel with the record of the American State. The German State is persecuting a minority, just as the American State did after 1776; the Italian State breaks into Ethiopia, just as the American State broke into Mexico; the Japanese State kills off the Manchurian tribes in wholesale lots, just as the American State did the Indian tribes; ... the imperialist French State massacres native civilians on their own soil, as the American State

did in pursuit of its imperialistic policies in the Pacific, and so on.[34]

Even today, democratic officials often do things that they have no right to do and that we have no duty to let them do. Many times there are no peaceful means to stop them. My thesis is that we may do to them whatever we may do to each other.

CHAPTER 2

Defensive Ethics

THE GENERAL FRAMEWORK

Lying, cheating, stealing, sabotaging an organization, destroying property, physical violence, and killing are wrong in most circumstances. In special circumstances, however, these actions are permissible. I may not kill for fun, but I may kill a kidnapper in self-defense. I may not lie for personal gain, but I may lie to save people from the murderer at the door.

In this chapter, I'll start by giving a brief overview of the ethics of defensive killing. The broad outline of this theory is largely uncontroversial, though the precise details might be so. That won't be a problem for the book's argument for two reasons. First, the controversy is over relatively small things, such as exactly how to interpret what counts as an "imminent threat" or whether there is a "proportionality" requirement on self-defense. These are real disputes, but they are more like arguing over whether the speed limit should be eighty or eighty-five miles per hour than whether we should ban automobiles. Second, all I am maintaining in this book is that governmental wrongdoers are on par with nongovernmental ones: the same principles that explain when we can use defensive resistance against the latter apply to the former. Thus, I don't need to settle on a precise view of what counts as an imminent threat or whether there are proportionality requirements because my point is just that whatever the truth of the matter is there, it applies to both types of wrongdoers. We don't have good reasons to treat civilian and government wrongdoers differently.

The principles governing defensive deception, sabotage, and destruction are largely the same as those governing defensive killing, except that they are less stringent because these actions are less harmful. I start with defensive killing because it's the hardest case.

In the end, I'll list a number of hypothetical cases of civilian wrongdoing in which we would normally judge it permissible to kill, lie to, or sabotage civilians, or destroy their property. I'll then produce parallel cases involving government agents. I'll end by asking what, if anything, justifies thinking these cases should be treated differently. The next five chapters will argue that the answer is *nothing*.

A THEORY OF DEFENSIVE KILLING

Let's begin with a sketch of a theory of defensive killing, taken from Jeff McMahan's *Killing in War*, which itself seems to come from the common law.[1]

By default, killing is presumed wrong. We presume people have a right to life. By default, we have a duty not to kill others. In commonsense moral thinking, however, the duty not to kill, right to life, and value of human life are *conditional*. In some realistic circumstances, killing is permissible or even obligatory. In general, morality sets a high bar when it comes to justifying the initiation of violence against peaceful, innocent, nonaggressors. Yet when it comes to justifying the use of violence against violent aggressors, the bar is much lower.

A person can become liable to be killed by performing certain wrongful or unjust actions. A person is liable to be killed when he is doing something deeply wrong, unjust, or harmful to others, and when killing him would serve a defensive purpose, such as self-defense, the defense of others, or to prevent him from causing greater injustice.

Defensive killing is also restricted by a doctrine of *necessity*: at minimum, when a nonlethal alternative is equally effective at stopping someone from committing injustice, it is not permissible to kill him. Whether the doctrine of necessity is stricter than that is a disputed detail; I'll return to this point later.

To guide your intuitions, think about case A. again:

A. Shooter in the Park

A masked man emerges from a black van holding a rifle. He starts shooting at children in a public park. Ann, a bystander, has a gun. She kills him before he kills any innocent children.

What are the principles that explain why Ann may kill the shooter?

One way to discover what commonsense moral thinking says about the ethics of killing is to examine English common law. As John Hasnas says, "The doctrines of self-defense and defense of others are doctrines that developed through the common law process that embody centuries of experience regarding how best to discourage violence and resolve violent disputes." The doctrines "represent what fifty generations of juries and judges believed to be a fair and proper response to [wrongful] attack."[2] The common law is in general a reliable guide to people's moral intuitions about permissible killing. Unlike statutory law, which generally reflects bureaucrats' or politi-

cians' interests, the common law largely tracks and codi-
fies people's commonsense moral intuitions.

The common law assumes people have a right to protect themselves and others against "unlawful" threats
such as assault, battery, rape, and murder.[3] According to
the common law doctrine of self-defense, one person (the
"killer") may justifiably kill another (the "adversary")
when all the following apply:

1. The killer is not the aggressor.

2. He *reasonably believes* he (or someone else) is in *imminent danger* of severe bodily *harm* from his adversary.

3. He reasonably believes that killing is *necessary* to avoid
this danger.[4]

Note that the common law regards meeting these conditions as *justifications*, not merely excuses, for homicide.
The distinction is that when one has an excuse, the law
considers the homicide wrongful, but one's liability may
be reduced. So, for instance, suppose a gunman forces me
to shoot another innocent person. Here my act of killing
might be excused, but it is not justified. It's wrong, but
I was acting under duress, and so am not worthy of full
blame or punishment. In contrast, when Ann shoots the
gunman in the park, her action is not wrong at all.

THE HARM AND IMMINENT DANGER PROVISOS

In common law, killing in self-defense is justified only
if the threat of harm is severe enough. I can kill you to
stop you from raping or dismembering me, but not to stop
you from throwing mud at me or flicking me once in
the ear.

In terms of both law and morality, there's no obvious sharp line between what threats count as severe or not severe enough to warrant killing. Regarding the moral issue, we could reasonably dispute how severe the threat to one's body must be to warrant killing, and also whether one can attack or kill others to defend one's property.[5] For instance, suppose a man threatens to burn down my house and destroy my car, but the only way I can stop him is to shoot him. It seems at least reasonable to think I may attack or kill him in defense of my property, if the damage he intends to do is severe enough. Yet people could reasonably dispute that, especially if I'm rich and have insurance. I won't take a stance either way here, but I just note this could be one area of controversy. The legal codes of most countries do not allow you to use deadly violence to defend your property; most say you can only use violence to defend people. (In contrast, these same legal codes allow cops to use violence to protect property.) Still, that's not obviously the correct *moral* view.

Further, the imminent danger proviso does not literally mean that a victim must wait until the last possible second to defend herself. Suppose you have been kidnapped and have good reason to think that the kidnapper will murder you on day six of captivity. You need not wait until the last second before he tries to slit your throat to fight back. You may fight back, using deadly force, from day one.

Just how imminent the danger must be is also a matter of reasonable dispute. I won't take a stance here in this book because doing so is unnecessary for my thesis. After all, my goal is to argue that the principles governing defensive killing apply equally to both private and governmental wrongdoers, so I needn't resolve intramural debates about the fine details of those principles.

THE REASONABLENESS PROVISO

The common law merely requires the killer to have a "reasonable belief" that deadly force is necessary to protect herself. The test here is whether a reasonable person might hold the belief, not whether it is impossible for a reasonable person to doubt the belief. For example, in one famous case, a member of a gang was harassing the defender. The gang member reached into his pocket. The defender reasonably believed that the gang member was reaching for a gun and so shot the gang member dead. It turned out he was not armed and was just reaching for a pack of cigarettes.[6] Nevertheless, the defender was exonerated by the doctrine of self-defense. The common law doesn't require the defender to know for sure that the adversary had a gun or be free of reasonable doubt. Rather, the common law holds that the defender was reasonably in fear of his life, that it was reasonable for him (though he couldn't be certain) to believe that the gang member was reaching for a weapon, and the burdens and risks from reasonable epistemic uncertainty should fall on the aggressor, not the defender.

Now some philosophers might dispute the reasonableness criterion and think it's too permissive. For instance, they might hold that it matters not just whether your belief that you need to use violence to defend yourself is reasonable but instead whether it is *correct*. Some philosophers argue that you are justified in using violence in self-defense only when violence is in fact required; if you reasonably but mistakenly believe it is required, then you are merely excused, not justified. I'll stick to the common law formulation (which holds that reasonable belief justifies rather than merely excuses), but if you disagree, you can still accept a slightly modified version of the arguments in this book.

THE NECESSITY PROVISO

The "necessary" proviso means there are no *good* alternatives to lethal force, not that there are *no* alternatives, period. Suppose, in the *Shooter in the Park* case, that Ann has three options:

1. Kill the shooter, which has a 95 percent chance of saving the children.

2. Use a smoke screen to help the children escape, which has only a 25 percent chance of being effective.

3. Try to wrestle the shooter to the ground, which has only a 25 percent chance of being effective and a good chance of getting her killed.

In this case, Ann may kill the shooter, even though other alternatives have a greater than zero chance of success. She isn't required to incur significant danger of harm on herself to save the shooter's life nor is she required to use a significantly less reliable nonlethal method instead of a much more reliable lethal one. When we say that Ann should use no more force than necessary, we don't mean it has to be impossible to stop him with nonlethal methods.
Suppose Ann had a fourth option:

4. Subdue the shooter in an *expensive* nonlethal manner, which has a 100 percent chance of stopping him, but that would cost someone (Ann, an innocent bystander, or the city) $1 million. For instance, suppose Ann could use nonlethal violence to stop the shooter from killing the children, but only by smashing a rare painting over his head.

It's at least reasonable to dispute whether Ann (or innocent bystanders or the innocent city) should have to bear such high monetary costs just to subdue the shooter, when killing is cheap. After all, the shooter caused the moral emergency. It's not obvious we owe it to him to sacrifice so much wealth just to preserve his life, especially when that wealth can be used for other valuable ends. If someone disagrees here, it is probably just because I made the amount of wealth destroyed in option 4 ($1 million) too low. If Ann could nonlethally subdue the shooter only by causing $10 billion in damage that the city would have to pay for, then subduing the shooter in a nonlethal way would come at the expense of other important concerns, such as providing public schools or medical care.

Finally, one crucial question about the necessity proviso concerns whether people have a "duty of retreat." In some jurisdictions, people are not allowed to use deadly force (or any force) to protect themselves or others if they (and the others) could simply escape. In other jurisdictions, people are allowed to stand their ground: they are not required to flee to prevent themselves from suffering harm. In many jurisdictions, the duty of retreat only applies to public places; for example, you are not required to flee when an assailant invades your home. There's an interesting moral question here. But I will not attempt to resolve it because it is an intramural dispute about the nature of defensive violence. Regardless of whether you accept the moral parity or special immunity thesis, you could go either way.

IS THERE A PROPORTIONALITY REQUIREMENT?

Some people, including some politicians and judges, believe that the right of self-defense is subject to a proportionality requirement. The idea is that when you are defending yourself or someone else, you must not inflict "disproportionate harm" to your adversary. Some legal jurisdictions allow assailants or their beneficiaries to collect against defenders who disproportionately harmed the assailants during an act of self-defense.

Usually, the proportionality requirement appears as part of tort law rather than criminal law. Suppose you are the aggressor and I am the defender. You try to cut off my hand, and in self-defense, I kill you. In most jurisdictions, this will be seen as justifiable homicide, and so I will not incur any *criminal* penalties. Yet in some of those same jurisdictions, your family might be able to collect damages against me, since I inflicted disproportionate harm; I killed you when you were merely going to cut off my hand.

So to summarize, in tort law, some US jurisdictions impose proportionately requirements on self-defense. If we use more force than the attacker is using on us, we can incur civil liability, if not criminal liability. My understanding is that the proportionately requirement was not originally part of the common law of torts but is instead a revision added later via statutes.

Heidi Hurd notes that this change in the law leads to what seem like absurd consequences. For instance, in some jurisdictions, if a woman kills her would-be rapist, she would face civil liability for damages since killing is out of proportion with rape.[7]

This is yet another part of the theory of self-defense where we might dispute the fine details. The basic and relatively uncontroversial idea is that you may not simply do anything it takes to defend yourself from threats. Rather, what you are permitted to *knowingly and intentionally* do to the assailant depends in part on what you reasonably believe the assailant is trying to do to you.

To take an example from Hurd, suppose I know that you plan to tap me once on my shoulder, despite my clear warning not to do so. Tapping my shoulder without my consent does not harm me, but it nevertheless violates my right to bodily integrity.

Now suppose I know you plan to tap me on the shoulder once. It seems I can swat your hand away. But suppose instead the only way I can stop you from tapping me is to kill you; I have no less-than-lethal means to preventing you from doing so. Hurd thinks it is plausible to conclude that I am not permitted to kill you but instead must suck it up and bear the unwanted tap on the shoulder, even though you act wrongly and violate my rights.[8]

The question of proportionality concerns how much harm the defender is permitted to inflict intentionally on the assailant to stop the assailant from violating the defender's rights in various ways. Consider the following table. On the left side, I have a list of increasingly severe actions a defender might undertake. On the right side, I have a list of more or less increasingly severe actions an assailant or adversary might commit that the defender tries to defend herself from. (In the right column, we might dispute the precise order of severity. I'm not asserting that rape is less bad than having one's hand cut off. Feel free to rearrange the order of the harms in whatever way you think reasonable.)

The question is: Given any known threat from the list on the right side, what may the defender intentionally do (from the left-hand column) to the assailant, assuming that this action is *necessary* (as defined above) to stop the assault? If you want, draw a green line between the actions from the left- and right-hand columns to indicate "permissible," and a red line to indicate "impermissible." Chances are, if we all do this exercise, we'll have slightly different sets of green and red lines at the end.

Proportionality

The **defender** may do this to the assailant:	If she reasonably believes it is necessary stop the **assailant** from doing this to her:
Push him	Tapping her shoulder
Punch him	Kissing her
Severely but not permanently injure him	Groping her
	Causing a minor and non-permanent injury
Permanently injure him	
Kill him	Severely but not permanently injuring her
	Raping her
	Severely and permanently injuring her
	Torturing her
	Murdering her

Hurd thinks the best overall theory of proportionality holds killing is permissible to stop severe rights violations, while only lesser violence is permitted for lesser rights violations. Of course, as our likely different ways of filling in the table above would illustrate, what counts as severe is up for dispute. It's clear that you may kill a person to stop him from raping you, but not to stop him from tapping you on the shoulder. Where to draw the line is unclear.

Once again, strictly speaking I take no stance on how to interpret the proportionality requirement, if there is one. My goal here is to argue that the moral rules governing self-defense against government agents are no stricter than the moral rules governing self-defense against private civilians.

KILLING BOSSES: MUST THE THREAT BE IMMEDIATE AND DIRECT?

In the *Shooter in the Park* case, the shooter is a direct, immediate threat to the innocent children. It's plausible, however, that it can also be permissible to kill someone even if he is an indirect, distant threat. Consider the following case:

Mastermind

Wilson is a criminal mastermind. He continually evades the police—he cannot be brought to justice. He has an army of hundreds of henchmen who do his bidding. Wilson himself has never killed anyone. His henchmen have killed others at his command. Ann knows Wilson will soon issue another kill order. But Ann—a former Marine sniper—shoots Wilson from afar, killing him before he issues his next order.

Wilson has not directly killed anyone himself, but as far as we know, neither did Mao Tse-tung, Stalin, Hitler, or most of the twentieth century's other so-called mass murderers. Yet it still seems permissible for Ann to kill him, just as Altman and Wellman say, "Surely, it would have been permissible for somebody to assassinate Stalin in the 1930s."[9]

Ann may kill Wilson because

1. Wilson poses a continuing *indirect* threat to innocent people.

2. It is wrong for Wilson to cause harm to others.

3. Killing Wilson ends his ability to threaten others.

4. Killing Wilson will disrupt a dangerous and threatening organization.

5. Attempting to prosecute Wilson through the legal system is likely to fail or backfire, or is too risky to demand that Ann undertake. She has no other effective means of stopping Wilson.

When we watch superhero movies, and we see the superhero kill the leader of the evil terrorist or criminal organization, we rarely judge the hero to have act wrongly. Sure, if the hero could easily apprehend the mastermind and bring him to justice, we would expect the hero to do so. But if the hero cannot, we do not usually judge it wrong for the hero to kill the mastermind, even if the mastermind has not himself ever directly performed the heinous crimes. Indeed, sometimes we worry about certain heroes who *refuse* to kill; their principled stance against killing frequently just means that certain villains can cause harm again and again.[10]

Now strictly speaking, in this book I don't have to take a stance on whether killing "masterminds" is permissible. Strictly speaking, all I will argue for is moral parity: under whatever conditions we can kill civilian masterminds—that is, when people order henchmen to perform unjust acts—the same moral principles apply to government masterminds.

MUST KILLING STOP THE THREAT?

Let's think about one further complication regarding defensive killing. In *Shooter in the Park* when Ann kills the shooter, this stops the threat. We can sometimes kill others, though, even when killing them is not *guaranteed* to stop the threat they pose.

To see why, imagine that an attacker is trying to kill children in the park. He is in the process of throwing a grenade at the children. Suppose Ann is only fast enough to shoot him midway through his throw. Because she fires so late, she has only a 50 percent of stopping him from killing the children, although she has 100 percent chance of killing him.

Here it still seems she may kill the attacker, though she has less than a 100 percent chance of success. I am not sure how high or low the chance of success must be; that is open to reasonable disagreement. (I think that she may kill him even if this has only a 1 percent chance of saving the children, but some others might reasonably insist on a higher number.) It will not matter for my argument here just how high the chances must be. The important point is that killing is in some cases permissible even if it is not guaranteed to end the threat. It just has to have a good enough chance of doing so.

Also, it seems killing can be permissible even if it merely *delays* the threat. Consider the following case:

School Bombers

Ann stumbles on terrorists who are about to bomb a school. Since there is no other effective and safe way to stop them, she kills them. Yet Ann knows there is another terrorist cell. She knows that the second cell will just bomb the same school a few hours (or days, weeks, or months) later. Suppose for whatever reason she cannot warn the school and stop the second bombing. Thus, all the children are doomed, though by killing the first cell of terrorists now, she buys them extra time.

Even in this case, it seems permissible to kill the terrorists. If we disagree here, it is probably just over *how much* extra time killing the first set of terrorists must buy for the children. I think it is permissible to kill the terrorists just to give the schoolchildren an extra billionth of a second of life, but you might perhaps demand that killing give them an extra day. At any rate, if we have this argument, we might accept the general principle: it can be permissible to kill a wrongdoer even if that only *temporarily* rescues the innocent.

FURTHER COMPLICATIONS

Shooter in the Park is a paradigmatic case for the theory of defensive killing. It's easy to judge that Ann may kill the shooter to protect others. He's a threat to innocent people, and killing him ends the threat. Philosophers, however, have also identified some harder cases.

For example, consider the problem of *nonresponsible threats*.[11] Suppose Bob is about to answer his cell phone. Bob does not know, and let's suppose has no possible way of knowing, that terrorists have hacked his phone. When Bob answers the phone, this will cause a bomb planted nearby to explode, killing many innocent people (but not Bob, who is out of range). Is it permissible to kill Bob?[12]

Or consider the problem of *innocent bystanders* and *innocent shields*. Suppose innocent bystanders surrounded the shooter in the park. Suppose if Ann attempts to shoot him, there is a good chance she would miss, and hence injure or kill one of the innocent bystanders. Or suppose the shooter holds a hostage in front of him as a shield. May Ann fire at the shooter in either case?

In academic philosophy, there is considerable controversy about what to say about these cases. Some think you may kill nonresponsible threats, innocent bystanders, and innocent shields in order to save yourself and others. Some add that you can, but only if that saves the most lives on net or minimizes the total amount of harm. (For instance, suppose Ann could throw a grenade at the shooter, killing him and two innocent bystanders, but if she does not do so, the shooter will kill ten innocent people.) Others may think you may never kill nonresponsible threats, innocent bystanders, or innocent shields, or only in highly exceptional cases. They dispute just when such killings are justified rather than merely excused.

SUMMARY

I bring up these complexities in order to note what's controversial and what's not. Most people would accept the broad outline of defensive killing given above. One person (the "defender" or "killer") may justifiably kill another (the "adversary") when the defender is not the aggressor, and he reasonably believes he (or someone else) is in imminent danger of severe bodily harm from his adversary and that killing is necessary to avoid this danger. But how to fill in the precise details of these principles is something we can reasonably dispute.

I introduce these complications to make readers aware of them and signal that I am also aware of them. My primary goal, though, is to say that the ethical principles regulating defensive actions against government agents are no more stringent than the principles regulating defensive actions against civilians. In this book, I will in general not take any stance on the finer points of these principles. My view is just that when government agents are nonresponsible threats, innocent bystanders, or innocent shields, you may treat them the same way you would treat civilians in the same roles. Whatever proportionality rule governs self-defense against private civilians applies to government agents. Whatever rules apply to defensive violence against indirect threats from civilians apply to indirect threats from government agents. And so on.

DEFENSIVE LYING

So far, we've confined our discussion to defensive killing and defensive violence against other people's bodies. Let's turn now to consider defensive lying. Commonsense morality and most major moral theories hold that lying is only presumptively wrong. The prohibition against lying does not apply in every circumstance.[13] In the right circumstances, a person is not merely *excused* in lying but is also *justified*.[14]

Consider the following case:

Murderer at the Door
Your friends, fleeing an ax murderer, hide in your basement. The ax murderer appears at your door and politely asks, "Might you be hiding people in your basement? I'd like to murder them, if you don't mind."

Almost everyone judges that in this case, you don't owe the murderer the truth. Indeed, it would be *wrong* to tell the murderer the truth: "I cannot tell a lie. My friends are downstairs." You may use whatever deceptive tactics are necessary. (A fortiori, as I discussed above, you may even kill the ax murderer if that's necessary to protect your friends.)

The murderer at the door is commonly regarded as a counterexample to certain moral theories. If some moral theory implies that it is *wrong* to lie to the murderer at the door, then the theory is for that reason and to that extent mistaken.

For instance, many people interpret Immanuel Kant's moral theory as implying that we cannot lie to the murderer at the door, although many Kant scholars think that's a misreading of Kant.[15] Still, if Kant's theory does indeed imply that we cannot lie to the murderer at the door, then it seems like a good reason to reject his theory. Kant's moral theory as a whole, his arguments for the theory, and many of Kant's premises are significantly less plausible than the claim that we may lie to the murderer at the door.

Of course, this considered judgment—that it is permissible to lie to the murderer at the door—could be mistaken. Perhaps some philosopher will produce a compelling argument showing us that lying is in fact wrong. But thus far no one has (Kant certainly hasn't), and so far no extant moral theory is itself more plausible than the claim that we may lie to the murderer at the door.

With this is mind, here is a sketch of a theory of *defensive lying*, which is itself modeled on the theory of defensive killing. By default, lying is presumed wrong. Yet a person can become *liable to be deceived* by performing (or intending to perform) certain deeply wrongful, harmful, or unjust actions. A person is liable to be deceived when he is doing (or intending to do) something deeply wrong, unjust, or harmful to others, or to prevent him from causing greater injustice. Defensive lying might also be governed by a doctrine of *necessity*: when a nondeceptive alternative is equally effective at stopping the wrongdoer from committing injustice, then perhaps it is wrong to lie. Further, whether defensive deception is merely permissible or obligatory might depend in part on whether the potential liar is in danger of retaliation or not. If I can lie with impunity to the murderer at the door, then I should, yet if the murderer at the door might try to kill me for lying, then lying is permissible (and heroic) but not required. I suspect most people accept this broad outline, even though they would dispute some of the exact details of any full theory of defensive lying, just as they dispute the fine details of defensive killing.

In general, if defensive lying and defensive violence are equally effective at stopping a wrongful aggressor from harming someone, then defensive lying is justified but defensive violence is not. Both defensive lying and defensive violence are governed by doctrines of necessity. Nevertheless, when choosing among equally effective defensive actions, one should pick the least harmful one. If you could somehow stop the shooter in the park by yelling "stop!" you should do that rather than lie to him. If you could stop him by lying as opposed to hurting him, you should lie. If you could stop him by shooting him in the leg versus the chest, you should shoot the leg. And so on. As I discussed above, there are trade-offs here. If lying has a small chance of stopping the shooter, but killing him has a high chance of success, one may kill him. When the chances of success are close, however, one should use the least violent and harmful means to stop the aggressor.

DEFENSIVE SABOTAGE, THEFT, AND DESTRUCTION

Defensive sabotage, theft, and destruction are governed by similar norms as defensive lying and violence against another's person. A defender may engage in sabotage against an aggressor, or may steal or destroy the aggressor's property, provided the defender reasonably believes that doing so is necessary to prevent the aggressor from committing a severe injustice.

For instance, suppose Ann knows the local mafia is trafficking child sex workers and routinely shakes down local businesses. Ann is a skilled hacker. She can hack into the mafia's computers and phones. When she does so, she can disrupt its communications, for example, by deleting e-mails, sending misinformation over e-mail, and the like. She can also steal its funds, which she might then redistribute to, say, the charity GiveDirectly. By doing so, she might not be able to stop the mafia altogether but she can significantly reduce the amount of injustice it does. This seems like justified sabotage.

Or suppose Ann knows that a particular car belongs to a local gang. Every night the gang gets in the car, drives around town until it finds a person walking alone, and then attacks that person. Ann decides one day, when no one's looking, to smash the car, slash the tires, cut the fuel line, and the like. As a result, the gang has to have the car repaired and refrains from hurting anyone for a few days. This seems like justified sabotage too. Suppose that finally Ann decides simply to destroy the car. Every time the gang gets a new car, she destroys that too. Again, this seems justified.

Again, these defensive actions are governed by doctrines of necessity. In general, one should engage in the minimal amount of theft or destruction to stop the crimes. In some cases, though, perhaps the wrongdoers in question might lack any sort of right to the property in their possession. There may be little reason in that case to minimize theft, destruction, or sabotage.

Typically, when choosing among defensive actions, one should pick the least harmful and violent action. Thus all things equal, lying is generally preferable to theft, sabotage, and destruction, which are in turn usually preferable to violence against another person. But again, the trade-offs here are subtle. As I explored above, this is not to say that a defender must choose nonviolent means with a low chance of success over violent means with a high chance of success.

EXAMPLE CASES OF RIGHTFUL DEFENSIVE ACTION

By now it should be clear that there are a great number of hard questions or disputed answers about the ethics of defensive action. There are difficult questions regarding how to think about proportionality, about just how severe a harm must be to warrant different kinds of defensive action, about how much risk a defender must accept, and just what counts as necessity, and so on. If my goal here were to give you a full theory of defensive action, I would try to resolve these disputes.

But that's not my goal. My goal is to convince you of the moral parity thesis, examine some implications of it, and think about some related issues. You and I can agree on just what necessity amounts to but dispute the moral parity thesis, or we might both accept the moral parity thesis but dispute the best understanding of the necessity proviso. What I've largely done above is simply sketched out the common core of the theory of defensive action that almost everyone accepts and then looked at the disputed details. As I think will become clear over the next few chapters, these disputes have little to no bearing on the moral parity or special immunity theses, or the main questions of this book.

With all that out of the way, let's construct a list of cases where defensive action of various sorts is permissible, according to the theory sketched above. Some of these we've seen before, and some are new. At the end of each case, I describe Ann committing a defensive action. In each case, this action seems permissible and indeed laudable. Ann is a hero.

A. Shooter in the Park

A masked man emerges from a black van holding a rifle. He starts shooting at children in a public park. Ann, a bystander, has a gun. She kills him before he kills any innocent children.

B. Drunk Partygoer

Rodney has too much to drink at a party. He runs around the house with a tiki torch, loudly yelling, "Look, everyone, I'm the Human Torch!" Four partygoers chase him outside to stop him from accidentally starting a fire. In their anger, they knock him down. They continuously kick his face and stomach, and beat him with bats and sticks. Ann sees that Rodney is subdued, and sees that the men beating him are carrying pistols, though they aren't using them. She pulls out her gun and yells for them to stop, but they ignore her. Finally, she pulls out her own weapon and shoots one of them in order to stop the beating as well as possibly save Rodney's life.

C. Health Nut

Health guru John sincerely believes that caffeine is unhealthy, causes laziness, and induces people to use hard drugs. John announces that in order to protect his neighbors and promote the social good, he and his followers will capture coffee drinkers, confiscate their belongings, and imprison them in John's filthy basement for years. Ann, who is too poor to move away from town, loves coffee. She secretly drinks it in the morning in her kitchen.

One day, a henchman breaks into her house and attempts to capture her. She struggles to defend herself, and in the process, kills him.

D. Terrorist

Cobra Commander, leader of the terrorist organization COBRA, uses a combination of bribes, subterfuge, and threats to get the leaders of the United States to do his bidding. He then gets the US military to perform an unjust invasion of another country. Ann, who is a private security guard, realizes that the individual she's protecting is secretly Cobra Commander and discovers his plot. Right before Cobra Commander issues an order that will kill hundreds of innocent civilians, she shoots him in the back of the head.

E. Mastermind

Wilson is a criminal mastermind. He continually evades the police; he cannot be brought to justice. He has an army of hundreds of henchmen who do his bidding. Wilson himself has never killed anyone. His henchmen have killed others at his command. Ann knows Wilson will soon issue another kill order. But Ann—a former Marine sniper—shoots Wilson from afar, killing him before he issues his next order.

F. Hacker

The local mafia has secretly been spying on everyone, stealing their personal information, recording their phone calls, and the like. The mafia also engages in a wide range of harmful and unjust activities. Ann hacks into its servers and makes the evidence that the mafia is doing such things public.

G. Vigilante Jailer

Bob, like many people in his town, believes that Ann might be a murderer and the government acts wrongly by refusing to try her. So one day, he kidnaps Ann and holds a trial for her in his basement. Bob is a fanatic believer in due process so he makes sure the trial looks like a normal one. He even grants Ann a defense lawyer and trial by jury. (They are not biased against Ann but instead just agree with Bob that the local government tends to fail to administer justice.) Ann is found guilty. Yet she is in fact innocent. As punishment, the jury decides that Ann should spend ten years locked in Bob's basement. At the first chance she gets, Ann makes a shiv, stabs Bob, and escapes.

H. Mafia Protection Money

The local mafia does many things. It engages in criminal activities, and often hurts or kills people that get in its way. In beats down and intimidates local businesspeople to get them to pay protection money. But it also dispenses justice from time to time by punishing people who wrongly hurt its clients, and distributing significant amounts of money to poor widows and families. Ann runs a small business. The amount of protection money the mafia demands from businesses depends on how successful the business is. Ann routinely lies about how much she makes, keeping some money off the books (which the mafia frequently audits) and keeping her wealth hidden away where the mafia can't find it.

I. Justice League Turned Bad

For the past twenty years, the Justice League has protected innocent people from supervillains and other threats. Indeed thus far, it is made up of the most heroic people who have ever lived, having saved the world at least a dozen times. Nevertheless, one day Superman, the leader of the Justice League, orders superhero Awesome Ann to use her psychic blast power to blow up an entire village. Superman explains, "I'm pretty sure Lex Luthor is hiding in

there. I want him dead. Collateral damage be damned."
Awesome Ann refuses. Superman shrugs, "Well, I'll just
get Wonder Woman to do it then." Ann uses her psychic
blast on Superman instead, killing or crippling him.

J. Saboteur

Ann knows the local mafia is trafficking child sex workers and routinely shakes down local businesses. Ann is
a skilled hacker. She hacks its computers and phones,
disrupts its communications, deletes e-mails, sends misinformation over e-mail, and the like. She also steals its
funds, donating them to the charity GiveDirectly.

K. Sneaky Recruit

Ann knows the local mafia is trafficking child sex workers and routinely shakes down local businesses. She manages to join the organization by tricking it into thinking
she's helping it complete its criminal activities. Over time,
she rises to become one of the leaders, all without actually doing anything criminal herself. Then when she has
a position of power, she orders her underlings to do
things that, in concert, destroy the organization, leading
to most of the members being arrested and the children
going free.

L. Secret Free Trader

Bob believes that buying Chinese imports is wrong. He
thinks we should buy American. He announces loudly,
"Henceforth, anyone who buys Chinese supplies for his
or her business has to pay a fine equal to 50 percent of
the costs of their imports, which I will then redistribute
to our fine working men and women in Michigan." For
whatever reason, the local law enforcement intends to
help Bob with his scheme. Ann runs a factory. When Bob
comes around to see if she's complied with his demands,

she tricks him into thinking she has. But she hasn't; in fact, she regularly buys from China.

M. Bomber

Ann knows that a particular car belongs to a local gang. Every night, the gang gets in the car, drives around town until it finds a person walking alone, and then attacks that person. Ann decides one day to burn the car when no one's looking.

And so on. We can construct endless cases just like these, in which Ann rightly uses deception, sabotage, destruction, or violence against another person or group of people, either to protect herself or others.

PARALLEL CASES WITH GOVERNMENT AGENTS

But what happens if we replace the wrongdoers from cases A–M with government agents doing more or less the same things? Consider the following:

A'. Minivan Shooter

Ann witnesses a police officer stop a minivan with a female driver and three children in the back. Ann sees that the driver has nothing in her hands and her hands are on the steering wheel. The police officer emerges from his car and starts shooting at the van's windows. Ann has a gun. She fires at the police officer before he shoots any of the children.

B'. Drunk Driver

Rodney, intoxicated after a night spent drinking, starts speeding on the highway. The cops try to pull him over. He ignores them, and then a high-speed chase ensues. When the cops finally pull him over, they do not merely yank him out of the car and arrest him. Rather, even after he is subdued and lying prostrate on the ground, they take turns clubbing him with their batons. Ann witnesses the beating and yells for them to stop. The cops ignore her. Finally, she pulls out her own weapon and shoots one of them in order to stop the beating as well as possibly save Rodney's life.

C'. War on Drugs

Town leaders decide to make marijuana illegal, even though there is overwhelming evidence that marijuana is in every respect less harmful than alcohol—a drug that is legal for any adult to consume. Ann has a pot stash in her house. One night, a bunch of police officers raid Ann's house in a no-knock raid. She recognizes that they are police officers. She also knows that if they capture her, she will be imprisoned for a decade. Her government issues overly punitive sentences for drug possession and is unresponsive to citizens' demands to overturn the law. Ann resists arrest and escapes.

D'. Hawk

Ann, a secret service agent, happens to be in the situation room when she hears the president order the unjust invasion of another country. Right before the president issues an order that——as the generals and other experts in the room make clear—will kill hundreds of innocent civilians, she knocks him out and subdues him.

E'. Chief Executive Mastermind

Walker is president. He initiates what is clearly an unjust war, though many people unreasonably believe it to be just. Under his command, the government kills tens of thousands of innocent civilians and soldiers in foreign countries. Thousands of domestic troops die in vain fighting Walker's wars. The war destroys massive amounts of property and wealth. Tens of thousands of civilians die from the war's fallout. Walker now plans to initiate another unjust war of the same sort in another country. Ann tries to use peaceful means to stop the war, but these fail. Ann intervenes. She kills Walker with a sniper rifle. As a result, this stops the next war, since Walker's successor is less belligerent.

F'. The Leaker

The government has secretly been spying on large numbers of people, stealing their personal information, recording their phone calls, and the like. The government also engages in a wide range of harmful and unjust activities. Ann hacks into its servers and makes the evidence that the US government is doing such things public.

G'. Regular Jailer

The district attorney, Bob, like many people in his town, believes that Ann might be a murderer. So one day, he gets the police to arrest Ann and holds a trial for her in the district court. Bob is a fanatic believer in due process so he makes sure Ann gets a proper trial. Ann is found guilty after a fair and proper trial. She is in fact innocent. As punishment, the jury decides that Ann will get life in prison. Ann's request for an appeal is turned down. At the first chance she gets, Ann makes a shiv, stabs a guard, and escapes.[16]

H'. Taxes

The US government does many things. It engages in many unjust activities, and often hurts or kills people that get in its way. But it also dispenses justice from time to time by punishing criminals and distributing significant amounts of money to poor families. Ann runs a small business. The amount of taxes she is supposed to pay depends on how profitable her business is. Ann routinely does not tell the truth about how much she makes, keeping some money off the books (which the US government frequently audits) and her wealth hidden away where the government can't find it.

I'. War Crime

For the past twenty years, the US military has protected innocent people from evil dictators and other threats. Indeed thus far, it has been made up of the most heroic soldiers who have ever lived, having saved the world from the Nazi scourge. Nevertheless, during one ill-advised war, a lieutenant orders his men to exterminate the women, children, and old men living in rural village. When they do so, helicopter pilot Ann intervenes. She instead rescues the villagers, and tells her crew members to fire their machine guns at any US army soldiers or villagers who try to stop them.

J'. National Security Agency Saboteur

Ann suspects the National Security Agency is wrongfully spying on people. She takes a job with a government contractor, gets security clearances, and then discovers, unfortunately, that she's right. She steals a number of documents revealing the agency's misbehavior, which she then turns over to a prominent investigative journalist. She flees the country to avoid arrest.

K'. District Attorney

Ann knows the government often criminalizes activities that it ought not to criminalize. She manages to be elected as the district attorney. While district attorney, she regularly engages in nullification, refusing to charge people who are caught doings that ought not be criminalized, such as possessing marijuana.

L'. Secret Free Trader

Voters believe that buying Chinese imports is wrong. They vote in a number of protectionist candidates for office. The new protectionist Congress announces, "Henceforth, anyone who buys Chinese supplies for his or her business has to pay a tariff equal to 50 percent of the costs of their imports, the funds from which will be used to fund social welfare programs." Ann runs a factory. When a government auditor comes around to see if she's complied with his demands, she tricks him into thinking she has. But she hasn't; in fact, she regularly buys from China. She never pays the tariff.

M'. Bomber

Ann lives near a local military base. She learns from a soldier that the US military repairs its tactical drones there before redeploying them. She learns that at least 90 percent of the people killed in drone strikes were not the intended targets of the attacks.[17] She sneaks onto the base and blows up the drones, using homemade bombs.

Each of the cases A'–M' is written to be more or less analogous to the cases A–M above, with the only major difference being that Ann is using defensive actions against government agents acting ex officio rather than against civilians. In each case, however, it looks at least at first glance that the government is committing the same injustices that the aggressors in A–M were committing. When Ann interferes, she either stops them or at least delays them in causing unjust harms.

If some defensive action is permissible in any of cases A–M, we should presume the same defensive action is also permissible in A'–M', at least until we have been given a reason to think otherwise. The difference between the cases cannot be as simple as "cases A'–M' involve the government, so that's the difference." Of course that's *a* difference. But the question is whether this descriptive difference makes any *moral* difference, and *why*. If someone judges that we should treat cases A–M differently from A'–M', arguing that defensive action is right in the former and wrong in the latter cases, then we need some good explanation. If we cannot produce any good explanation despite repeatedly trying, then we should probably conclude there is no real difference.

In the next few chapters, I'll examine the best arguments on behalf of the special immunity thesis, which holds that the set of conditions under which we may use defensive action against government agents acting ex officio is much more tightly constrained than the conditions under which we may use defensive action against civilians. Chapter 3 rebuts arguments that try to ground special immunity on the supposed legitimacy and authority that some governments enjoy. Chapter 4 examines and debunks a range of other assertions for special immunity.

Before moving on, it's important to offer a clarification and note of warning. I agree with most sensible people that violent revolution is rarely a good idea. Most likely, any attempted revolution will fail. Even if it "succeeds" in overthrowing the current government, it is likely to lead to chaos and internal war, as the normal governmental mechanisms in place to ensure people's safety break down. Further, people dependent on welfare or social security payments will be greatly harmed. Finally, it's almost impossible to overthrow a government without harming great numbers of innocent people.

But advocating *defensive actions* against, including in some cases violent resistance to, government injustice is not the same thing as advocating violent revolution. To say that it can be right to use lethal force against a law enforcement official who uses excessive force is not to say, and does not commit one to claiming, that the entire government should be overthrown. To justify *revolution* is to justify war. It's one thing to assassinate a warmongering leader. It's another to overthrow the government altogether.

CHAPTER 3

The Government Authority Argument for Special Immunity

In the previous chapter, we discussed a general framework for defensive actions. Certain actions, such as lying, deceiving, cheating, stealing, destroying, attacking, and killing, are usually wrong. But one person (the defender) is permitted to perform these actions against an adversary or his property provided that the defender is not the aggressor, the defender reasonably believes that he or someone else is in imminent danger of being a victim of severe injustice or harm, and he reasonably believes that using the defensive action is necessary (and perhaps proportional) to protect himself or others from those severe injustices or harms. As we saw, there is reasonable debate about just how to fill in the details, such as how to interpret the reasonable belief, imminent danger, proportionality, and necessity provisos. My argument doesn't require me to take a stand on those issues, so I don't.

We also saw that it's easy to construct cases where these conditions apply not only to private agents but also to agents of democratic governments. Yet many people have different judgments in these two cases. They thus appear to subscribe to the special immunity thesis.

In this chapter, I explore and debunk what appears to be the obvious justification for the special immunity thesis. There is a widespread view that governments, or at least democratic governments, have a special moral status. Unlike lone shooters, criminal organizations, health nuts, murderers at the door, or totalitarian dictators, many democratic governments (and by extension, their agents acting ex officio) are both *legitimate* and *authoritative*. They have a right to rule, and we have a duty to obey them. Therefore, while it is permissible to attack an evil-doing terrorist, it is not permissible to attack an evil-doing president, even when that president and the terrorist seem to be doing the same thing.

THE CONCEPTS OF AUTHORITY AND LEGITIMACY

To evaluate this purported justification of the special immunity thesis, we must first clarify what the terms "legitimacy" and "authority" mean. Governments generally claim to have two moral powers that ordinary people lack. To illustrate this, consider the following four cases:

1. Virtuous Vani believes Americans are becoming too fat. She arrives at a 7-Eleven store brandishing a gun and declares, "From now one, no one may purchase Big Gulps. Big Gulps are bad for you. If you want to drink that much soda, you must purchase a smaller drink, and then return, and purchase another drink when it's empty. I'm sorry, people, but this is for your own good!"

2. Principled Peter believes Americans should not live high while other people die. He believes that we are all in this together. He hacks into upper-middle-class and rich people's bank accounts, and then redistributes their wealth to poor people.

3. Decent Dani believes Americans should support one another and prioritize each others' welfare over that of

foreigners. He notices that high-income people seem far too eager to buy German as opposed to US luxury cars. He shows up at a BMW dealership brandishing a gun and says, "Listen here. When you buy a 3 Series, you're helping employ strangers in Munich rather than your fellow citizens in Lansing or Detroit. So here's the deal. I'll let you buy these cars, but only if you pay me an extra $3,000, which I will use to help your fellow citizens, whom you clearly don't care about."

4. Enterprising Elon believes space exploration is a vital project. Accordingly, he builds elaborate and expensive satellites, probes, telescopes, and shuttles, and then sends each American a small bill, proportional to their income. When they refuse to pay, he hacks into their bank accounts and garnishes their wages.[1]

If Vani, Peter, Dani, or Elon were to do these things, we would probably call the police and demand that they be arrested. The police would indeed show up and arrest or perhaps even use force against them.

But there's a puzzle here. While we think Vani's, Peter's, Dani's, and Elon's actions are criminal, our own governments do these same things. What's perplexing in a sense is why people don't find that puzzling. They believe that governments are permitted to do things ordinary people are forbidden from doing. In particular, they believe that governments are permitted to issue commands telling us what to do and not to do, and that the governments may use violence and threats of violence to make us comply with these commands. Furthermore, people believe that we are morally obligated not to stop governments from acting like Vani, Peter, Dani, or Elon. We must instead obey our government when it acts like Vani, Peter, Dani, or Elon.

Governments claim to possess two special moral powers:

1. The permission to create and enforce rules over certain people within a geographic area.

2. The ability to create in others a *moral obligation* to obey those rules.

I'll call the first power *legitimacy* and the second power *authority*.

A Note on Definitions: the use of these terms "legitimacy" and "authority" is not standardized in political philosophy.[2] Some philosophers use the terms the way I do. Others use them the opposite way, or use authority or legitimacy to refer to both powers combined.[3] Nothing substantive hinges on what words we use. Everyone whom I'll be debating here recognizes that the two moral powers of interest are the purported ones. I will use these words a particular way, but some of the philosophers whom I refer to might use different terms in their own writings. To avoid confusion, I'll just reword their arguments using these stipulated definitions above.

With that aside, let us get back to the concepts. A government is legitimate just in case it is permissible for that government to create, issue, and enforce rules using coercion. A government is authoritative, or has authority, over certain people just in case those people have a moral duty to obey that government's laws, edicts, and commands. Legitimacy is the power that could make it permissible for the government to tax you. Authority is the power that could make it impermissible for you to refuse to pay your taxes. Legitimacy makes it OK for the police to arrest you. Authority makes it wrong for you to resist them when they try to arrest you. In short, "legitimacy" refers to something like the moral permission to coerce, while "authority" refers to a moral power that induces in others a duty to submit and obey.

Importantly, for a government to have authority, it must be able to *create* obligations where there were none previously. Or more precisely, it must have the power to create an additional *source* of or *reason* for obligation where there was none previously. By definition, if the government has authority over a person, then when the government commands that person to do something, she has a moral duty to do it (at least in part) *because* the government says so.

Suppose I were to stand in Times Square and shout to people, "I command you not to kill one another (except in self-defense or the defense of others)." People would indeed have a duty to act in accordance with my command. But they would not specifically have a duty to *obey* me. Rather, they have preexisting and independent moral obligations not to kill one other. I would simply be commanding them to do something they already have a duty to do. One of them could say, "Listen, we acknowledge we have a duty not to kill each other, but we don't have any such duty *because* you said so. When you 'command' us not to kill each other, this does not give us any further reason not to kill each other." My command is morally *inert*: it does not create or enhance people's obligations in any way; it does not give them any additional reason to forbear from killing one another.

In contrast, most people who believe in government authority believe it can create additional grounds of obligation when it issues commands, edicts, laws, and so on. Again, we have preexisting moral obligations not to kill each other. Even if the government told me it would never prosecute me for murder, I would still have a moral duty not to murder people. Believers in government authority, however, usually hold that when the government criminalizes murder, this gives citizens an *additional*, weighty, and on its own sufficient moral reason not to murder people. When the government outlaws murder, I have a duty not to murder both because there are independent, extralegal reasons not to do so and the government told me not to.

In some cases, a believer in government authority holds that by issuing commands, a government does not just add new reasons for abiding by already-existing duties but also can *create* duties out of thin air. For instance, suppose there is no independent moral obligation to avoid drinking absinthe. But now suppose the government *authoritatively* forbids me from drinking it. In that case, I would suddenly have a duty not to drink absinthe. The government *creates* this duty by virtue of issuing a command (through some privileged legal process).

In summary, a believer in government authority has to believe at least one of the two following views:

A. In some cases, a government can create additional grounds for preexisting obligations by virtue of issuing a command (law, edict, regulation, etc.).

B. In some cases, a government can create additional obligations by virtue of issuing a command (law, edict, regulation, etc.).

DISPUTED QUESTIONS ABOUT LEGITIMACY AND AUTHORITY

By definition, a government is legitimate just in case it is permissible for that government to create, issue, and coercively enforce rules. Yet this definition leaves open a number of substantive questions, which every theory of government legitimacy will have to settle:

1. What determines whether a government has legitimacy or not?

2. Does any government in fact have legitimacy?

3. What is the *scope* of government legitimacy? That is, about which issues may a government create rules? For example, liberals standardly believe that it is outside the scope of government legitimacy to forbid you from having sex with another consenting adult. Libertarians believe it is outside the scope of government legitimacy to make an adult wear a seat belt while driving. Some conservatives think it is outside the scope of government to teach children evolutionary biology. Fascists and totalitarian communists think everything is within the scope of government.

4. *How* may government enforce the rules? Few people think that a government may execute all lawbreakers on their first offense. Instead, there are many complicated questions about what is the best and most just way to enforce the rules.

5. What is the *range* of a government? That is, over which people does a particular government permissibly create and enforce rules. For instance, suppose the US government says, "We are criminalizing marijuana use around the world. We plan to imprison for two days anyone anywhere who uses pot." Is that permissible, or may the US government only enforce this law among its own citizens?

In short, the concept of government legitimacy refers to the power to permissibly create and enforce rules, but differing conceptions or theories of legitimacy clash over the answers to these questions.

By definition, a government is authoritative (or "has authority") over certain people just in case those people have a moral duty to obey that government's laws, edicts, and commands. Analogous questions arise for authority as they do for legitimacy:

1. What determines whether a government has authority or not?

2. Does any government actually have authority?

3. What is the proper scope of government authority?

4. How strong is the duty to obey? (How easily can that duty be trumped or outweighed by contrary considerations?)

5. What is the proper range of government authority?

Authority is the moral power to create obligations through issuing commands. But different theories of authority will answer these substantive questions differently.

Both an anarchist and statist, and both the libertarian and totalitarian, can thus accept the definitions of legitimacy and authority I've offered here. For them, the dispute is whether any governments in fact have either moral power, and how much of that power the government has. Their dispute isn't over what the terms mean but rather over the answers to these two sets of questions.

LEGITIMACY AND AUTHORITY ARE INDEPENDENT PROPERTIES

Legitimacy and authority are *independent* moral properties. Most theories of legitimacy and authority try to ground both properties on the same principles, such that governments have both or neither. But at least as a matter of logic, a government (or any other rule-making entity) could have one without the other. Having legitimacy does not suffice to have authority; having authority does not suffice to have legitimacy. At least as a matter of logic, a government could be legitimate but not authoritative, or authoritative but not legitimate. Since legitimacy and authority are different moral powers, it's at least coherent to hold that governments have one but not the other.

To illustrate how a government-like entity could be authoritative but not legitimate, imagine a theory of authority called "pacifist monarchism." This hypothetical political theory holds that we are each duty bound to obey our queen. This theory forbids all violence and coercion, though. The queen may not coerce people into following her commands. She may not employ a military or police force. She may not use violence even to stop others from acting violently. This hypothetical political theory holds that the queen is authoritative but not legitimate. This theory may be silly, yet it is also coherent; it contains no logical contradiction.

It is similarly coherent to believe that governments could be legitimate but not authoritative. That is, it's coherent to hold that a government might have moral permission to stand and create laws, even if no citizens have the duty to obey or defer to that government. The government would have permission to force citizens to obey, but citizens would have no obligation to obey. (To be more precise, we'd have no duty to obey the rules *because* the government orders us to do so, though we might still have independent reasons to obey the rules.) So for instance, one might hold that governments may permissibly tax citizens, but still hold that citizens have no duty to comply and could feel free to engage in tax evasion if they can get away with it. A view like this might be mistaken, but it's not incoherent.[4]

On the contrary, as I'll discuss below, there's reason to think this view—that governments have legitimacy but not authority—may now be the dominant position among political philosophers who write about authority and legitimacy. There are some strong reasons to think that some governments are legitimate, although as I'll show shortly, it turns out that whether governments are legitimate or not will have little bearing on the moral parity thesis. Nevertheless, there's little reason to think any governments are authoritative, as it looks like every major argument for government authority fails rather badly, and we may just be psychologically disposed to see authority everywhere even when there's no such thing.

THE IRRELEVANCE OF GOVERNMENT LEGITIMACY

For the sake of argument, let me grant the following position:

The Super-Duper Democratic Legitimacy Thesis

A democratic electorate may legitimately do whatever it damn well pleases. It may even implement horrifically unjust policies. For instance, the democratic majority may legitimately suspend all civil liberties and place everyone in a pain amplifier for eternity if it so desires. A democratic government may, by mere fiat, acquire moral permission to do anything to anyone at any time.

Now, the super-duper democratic legitimacy thesis is absurd, and no one believes it. As we'll see, however, I could grant the super-duper democratic legitimacy thesis and yet my argument for the moral parity thesis could still go through.

The reason I can grant that democratic governments may legitimately do as they please, without thereby undermining the moral parity thesis, is that once we distinguish correctly between authority and legitimacy, it turns out legitimacy has little bearing on whether it's permissible to resist government. Even if super-duper democratic legitimacy were correct, it would remain an open question whether one can sometimes or even always lie to the electorate, kill presidents, destroy government property, or sabotage government finances.

By definition, if a government has legitimacy to do X, then it has (at least under some circumstances) moral permission to use violence to enforce its ability to do X. If a government has legitimacy to issue rule X, then by definition it has moral permission to force and coerce you to comply with X. Yet as we just discussed in the last section, the fact that a government has legitimacy to do X, or force you to do X, does not imply citizens must let the government do X or obey the government when it does X. Legitimacy and authority are independent properties, and a government could conceivably have one but lack the other. That a government legitimately does X tells us nothing by itself about what citizens may or may not do in response. Citizens might instead have no duty to obey. They may even be free to resist, lie, or even fight back violently.

One way to illustrate this is to think of a boxing match. In a boxing match, both boxers have permission to punch each other. We might thus say that in a boxing match, punching is legitimate. But neither boxer has an obligation to *let* the other hit him. Each boxer can feel free to duck, block, and evade the others' punches. So neither boxer has the *authority* to punch, though punches are *legitimate*. So it might conceivably be with government: perhaps certain governments legitimately create and enforce rules, but no one has a duty to obey those governments.

GOVERNMENTS PROBABLY DON'T HAVE ANY AUTHORITY, PERIOD

Democratic legitimacy does not do the work that the defender of special immunity needs it to do. Instead, what may be of use in defending the special immunity thesis is that moral power I call authority.

One of the possible justifications for the special immunity thesis goes like this: at least some government agents enjoy special immunity because at least some governments are authoritative. According to this argument, we have a duty not to resist government agents, even when we would be able to resist private civilians acting the same way, because we have a general duty to obey governments agents (acting ex officio) and a duty to the law.

There's a serious problem, however, with invoking democratic authority to defend the special immunity thesis: there's strong reason to believe that *no* governments, democratic or otherwise, have *any* authority. The doctrine of government authority has been subjected to sustained and overwhelming philosophical criticism over the past thirty years. Following A. John Simmons's seminal work on political obligation, the dominant view among political philosophers who work on this topic now appears to be that certain governments have legitimacy (as I've defined it) but not authority.[5] (Or more precisely, they might have authority over a tiny subset of their citizenry.) After reviewing the literature, Michael Huemer similarly concludes, "Skepticism about political obligation [i.e., authority] is probably the dominant view" in philosophy now.[6] As Leslie Green says in his *Stanford Encyclopedia* article surveying the field, "There are plausible objections to each of the dominant justifications for the duty to obey the law.... Each leaves significant gaps in the authority of law."[7] Ned Dobos similarly concludes that "there is today a growing consensus to the effect that no theory of political obligation succeeds."[8]

While the belief in a duty to obey the law is widespread, a duty to obey the law probably isn't some basic moral duty, like the duty to avoid hurting people for fun. Rather, it's something of a mysterious duty (if it is a duty at all), because the duty to obey the law or government implies that *other* people can either impose on us or even relieve us of duties or rights by *fiat*. Over the past twenty-five hundred years, philosophers have produced many theories trying to explain why governments might have authority and why there would be a duty to obey the law. While a few contemporary philosophers are convinced by their own work, I think it's safe to say no theory has gained widespread acceptance, and it's clear that most of the major theories of authority have gaping holes. To review this literature would take an entire book.[9] Here I'll just summarize some of the flaws with some of the major theories.

ACTUAL CONSENT THEORY

For instance, one popular theory (among laypeople, if not philosophers) is that governments have authority over us because we consent to their rule. In particular, we've made a kind of contract with them: they agree to provide us with certain benefits, and we in turn agree to obey the rules and pay our taxes. The problem with this theory, though, is that our relationship to government does not appear to have *any* features that signify consent. Our relationship to government is no more analogous to a consensual contract than a red elephant is analogous to the number three.

To illustrate this, recently I purchased a Music Man Majesty guitar from Guitar Center. This was a stereotypical consensual transaction.[10] Each of the following features obtained:

A. I performed an act that signified my consent. In this case, I told salesperson Kelly, "I'll buy the Majesty."

B. I was not forced to buy the guitar and had a reasonable way of opting out. It's not as though Sterling Ball (the owner of Music Man guitars) was threatening to hurt my children if I didn't buy the guitar.

C. Active dissent would have stopped the deal. Had I said, "I tried the guitar and don't want it," that would have been the end of the story. It's not as though Kelly would have taken my money anyway.

D. Kelly was not allowed to take my money unless she gave me the guitar; Guitar Center had to hold up its end of the deal.

If we remove any one of these four conditions, the transaction would no longer have been consensual. Suppose, instead of A, that Guitar Center sends me the guitar and takes my money, even though I never said I wanted it. That's not consent; it's a weird form of theft. Suppose, instead of B, that Guitar Center employees put a gun to my head, and then tell me I must buy the guitar or die. That's not consent; it's robbery. Suppose, instead of C, that Guitar Center sends me the guitar even though I said I don't want it. That's not consent; that's an unwanted gift. If the store takes my money even though I said I didn't want the guitar, it's a form of theft. Suppose, instead of D, Kelly the salesperson takes my money, but keeps the guitar. That's not consent; that's fraud or breach of contract.

The problem with the actual consent theory is that our relationship with government looks much more like these cases of theft, robbery, unwanted gifts, or fraud and breach of contact than it does like a case of a consensual relationship. Regarding A, there is no plausible moment or action you perform that signifies consent. You don't sign a social contract the way you sign a mortgage or marriage contract. Regarding B, we have no reasonable way of opting out of our governments' rule. Most of us lack the power or even right to move to other countries, and governments control all the habitable land. You either submit to your government's rule or you die. Regarding C, governments impose their rules on us regardless of whether we actively dissent. Regarding D, as Huemer notes, US courts have repeatedly ruled that the government has no duty to protect individual citizens. Suppose you call the police to alert them that an intruder is in your house, but the police never bother to dispatch someone to help you and as a result the intruder repeatedly rapes you. The government still requires you to pay taxes for the protection services it chose not to deploy on your behalf.[11]

HYPOTHETICAL CONSENT THEORY

In response, many philosophers, such as Thomas Hobbes, have proposed "hypothetical consent theories," which say that governments have authority because we *would* agree to obey them under certain hypothetical conditions.

But there are a huge number of fatal problems with such theories. First, we generally only think hypothetical consent matters in cases when we cannot check to see whether a person actually consents. For instance, if you come into the emergency room unconscious, doctors will treat you because they assume you would consent to treatment if you could. Should you wake up, though, and with full control of your faculties, say, "Leave me alone; I don't want treatment," they have to stop.

Second, hypothetical consent theories at best usually seem to show only that it would be *unreasonable* or *irrational* for you not to agree; they do not demonstrate that it is obligatory. Suppose, for example, it's true that if you were perfectly well informed and perfectly motivated by a sense of fair play, you would sell me your car for $1,000. It doesn't follow that you are obligated to sell me the car, or that I may force you to sell it.

One further problem with both hypothetical and actual consent theories of authority is that they seem to misunderstand what promises, real or hypothetical, can do. Suppose I declare, "In exchange for my parents having provided me with benefits, I promise to obey them in all things." Now suppose my parents order me to murder some foreigners or throw their pot-smoking neighbors in the basement. Even though I did in fact promise to obey my parents, it's clear I don't acquire the duty to murder the foreigners or imprison the neighbors. Promises to perform *immoral* actions are invalid; I cannot acquire permission to do something evil just by promising to follow someone else's commands. In chapter 5, I'll return to this point, explaining why even soldiers and officers who explicitly promise to obey orders retain permission to disobey and resist unjust orders and rules.

Thus, one cannot defend the special immunity thesis on the basis of actual or hypothetical consent. As I'll discuss at greater length later in this chapter, defenders of special immunity cannot just appeal to general government authority. Rather, they have to argue that governments specifically have the authority to commit severe injustices and evils—the very injustices and evils we would be permitted to resist (using deception, sabotage, or violence) if private civilians perpetrated them. It won't be enough for believers in special immunity to show we have a duty to pay fair taxes and obey fairly posted speed limits. Instead, they'll need to show that when a police officer uses excessive violence, we have a duty to *let* him.

FAIR PLAY THEORY

Another major theory of authority, devised by H. L. A. Hart, holds that authority arises out of a duty of fair play: "When a number of persons conduct any joint enterprise according to rules and thus restrict their liberty, those who have submitted to those restrictions when required have a right to a similar submission from those who have benefited by their submission."[12] The idea here is that when some people incur a sacrifice to public goods that benefit all, the other people who benefit have a duty to contribute to those goods as well. It would be unfair of them to free ride on the public goods when others are sacrificing to provide them.

There are a large number of known problems with this argument. Robert Nozick illustrates one with his "public address system" thought experiment. He asks you to imagine that your neighbors create a public entertainment system, with loudspeakers throughout your neighborhood. Each neighbor takes turns playing songs, reciting poetry, conducting interviews, or whatnot. You enjoy the system. One day, let's say day 138, they come to you and say that it's *your* turn to spend the day entertaining people. Must you do so? Most people conclude no: even though you benefited from the system, you aren't duty bound to participate in it. Part of the reason for this judgment seems to be that you had no good way of *avoiding* receiving the benefits—you couldn't opt out without great expense to yourself. But this seems to hold for most of the benefits the state provides as well.

But let's say you find Nozick's objection unpersuasive, and you think Hart has provided a good argument for showing you have to "do your part" or pay your taxes. You still cannot easily defend the special immunity thesis using Hart's argument. It's unclear how Hart's argument would prove, specifically, that you have a duty to obey any random law, or more specifically, a duty to *defer* to government agents who commit injustice, or a duty to abdicate the right of self-defense or the defense of others. Hart's argument may offer a good rationale for explaining why we should pay fair taxes for police protection or agree to serve on juries when our name is selected. Yet it seems bizarre to say, "You benefit from some of the public goods the state supplies. In order to avoid unfairly free riding on the efforts of others to provide those public goods, you must not only pay taxes and serve on a jury when called but also must allow the president to exterminate and forcibly relocate Native American tribes. You must let police choke, subdue, and handcuff men in ways that result in their death. You must allow Congress to wage war against whomever it likes. You must allow the police to arrest you for smoking pot or selling Big Gulps." Those things have nothing to do with paying your fair share, playing fair, or avoiding free riding.

SUMMARY

These are just three of the major theories of authority. There are many others. Without reviewing them here, I just note, and think the proponents of the other theories would agree, that each of the theories has major holes.

Now even if all the major theories for government authority fail, that does not by itself suffice to prove that governments lack authority. There's a certain point, however, at which the consistent failure to prove X starts to become evidence that not-X. The belief that governments enjoy authority is widespread; even people living under illiberal and highly corrupt regimes tend to think their governments are legitimate and authoritative. Nevertheless, if governments do indeed have authority, it seems like there should be some morally relevant property or set of properties that explains *why* governments have authority. (Everyone agrees that it can't just be that "the property of being a government" is what confers authority.) If there is such a property, then it seems plausible that people should be able to identify it. But over the past twenty-five hundred years, a large number of highly qualified people have spent a large amount of effort trying but failing to identify that property.[13]

Further, we have good grounds to think that people would believe in government authority even if governments have no such authority. Empirical work generally finds we have a psychological bias to ascribe authority to others, even in cases where there clearly isn't any.[14]

Governments do everything in their power to reinforce that bias.

Perhaps that's wrong. Perhaps some governments really do have authority, and we just haven't been able to figure out why. But as we're about to see, even if governments do have a general kind of authority, it will take extra work to show that such authority would justify the special immunity thesis.

AUTHORITY ISN'T ALL OR NOTHING

Suppose, contrary to what seems to be the state of the philosophical literature, that democratic governments do in fact have some sort of authority. Even if heroically this were established, it takes *even* more work to defend the special immunity thesis on the basis of authority.

A government can have authority over some issues without having complete authority over everything. Indeed, probably every extant believer in democratic authority thinks that democratic governments have only a limited scope of authority. In the United States, hardly · anyone thinks the government has authority over *everything*. For instance, suppose the US government commands all to convert to Catholicism. Conservatives would say we have no duty to obey *that* law and would continue to say that even if the First Amendment were repealed. Suppose the government commanded us to avoid homosexual sex. Liberals would say we have no duty to obey that law.

Or perhaps they would say that the duty to obey is outweighed by contrary considerations. Even if we suppose the government has some general authority over many issues, this authority might only be presumptive rather than absolute. Perhaps democratic authority could be outweighed by contrary considerations or stronger obligations, such as an obligation to protect others from severe harm.

Even if most people believe (I think mistakenly) that there is a general duty to obey the law, they do not think that literally every law, edict, regulation, or command that a (democratic) government might issue is, all things considered, authoritative.

Recall from the previous chapter that on the common-sense theory of defensive action, violence, deception, sabotage, and destruction in self-defense and the defense of others are warranted to protect oneself or others from *severe* harm or injustice. To defend the special immunity thesis on the basis of authority, one must show that democratic government agents specifically have authority to commit severe harms or injustices—the very harms and injustices that would render a civilian liable to defensive action. For the special immunity thesis to be true, it's not enough that governments have some authority, like the authority to set speed limits or collect taxes for genuinely necessary public goods, but instead that all things considered, they have the *specific* authority to commit these severe injustices.

With that in mind, consider that each of the following could succeed or fail in being legitimate or authoritative:

1. Regime types as a kind. (For example, can a theocracy ever be legitimate or have authority?)

2. A particular government's overall right to stand. (For instance, is the US government legitimate or authoritative overall?)

3. Particular offices or branches within a government. (For example, is the Federal Reserve, Drug Enforcement Ad-

ministration, or Department of Homeland Security legitimate or authoritative?)

4. Particular government practices and procedures. (Is, say, judicial review, jury trials, or the indefinite detention of so-called enemy combatants legitimate or authoritative?)

5. Particular laws, commands, and regulations. (For instance, is marijuana criminalization in the United States legitimate or authoritative? Were the Comstock Laws legitimate or authoritative?)

6. Particular actions and decisions. (Was the *Dred Scott v. Sanford* decision authoritative? Was it legitimate to wage the Spanish-American War? Did citizens have a duty to let the government fight the war? Was the Indian Removal Act of 1830 legitimate or authoritative?)

These distinctions make a difference. Authority in one does not imply authority in another. A lack of authority in one need not imply a lack of authority in another.[15] Similarly, debates about legitimacy and authority are often taking place at different levels of generality. For example, Rawls's *Theory of Justice* or David Estlund's *Democratic Authority* contain lengthy discussions about what political and economic regimes as a *kind* are legitimate and authoritative. They focus almost entirely on the first issue, but they leave open most of the other ones.

Anyone who wants to defend the special immunity thesis on the basis of government authority has a serious burden. It won't be enough to justify a general kind of government authority. Instead, one must produce a theory that justifies granting democratic officials the *specific authority* to commit severe injustices—the kinds where we could justifiably use violence, subterfuge, or deception against civilians if the civilians were to try to commit them.

To illustrate this burden, imagine that Bill is the lawfully elected president. Suppose Bill is the authoritative president of what is overall an authoritative regime. But now imagine Bill demands sex from an intern. It seems obvious that even if Bill is authoritative overall, he does not have the authority to demand sex from interns. The intern has no duty to comply with his demands. Should he try to force her to have sex, she may, if necessary, use violence (including deadly violence) to protect herself. Until I see a compelling argument for a theory that says otherwise, I'd regard it as a reductio of any purported theory of authority that the intern must submit to Bill's demand for sex.

But that seems like an easy case, because Bill was not acting ex officio in his capacity as president. So let's look at another case. Suppose a sheriff, following the Fugitive Slave Act, arrests an escaped slave in the antebellum United States. Suppose I shoot the sheriff in order to free the slave. Even if we suppose that the US government in the 1850s was legitimate and authoritative overall, it seems deeply implausible to hold that citizens had a duty specifically to let it enforce slavery. Until I see a compelling argument for a theory that says otherwise, I'd regard it as a reductio of any purported theory of authority that it implies I must let sheriffs enforce slavery.

Or suppose the United States conducts a referendum on whether it will nuke the tiny island nation of Tuvalu. Suppose all eligible US voters vote. Suppose each of them, except me, votes to nuke Tuvalu. Suppose I know that there are no good grounds to nuke Tuvalu. In this case, it seems obvious that I have no duty to defer to my government leaders or fellow citizens when they attempt to nuke Tuvalu. Now perhaps someone will one day prove that according to the correct theory of government authority, democratic governments specifically have authority to nuke other countries for no good reason. At least until I see the compelling argument, though, I'd regard it as a reductio of any purported theory of authority that it implied this.

So invoking general government authority is not enough to justify the special immunity thesis. Someone trying to defend special immunity on the basis of authority faces a double burden. The objector must not only show that democratic governments have a kind of general authority but also must specifically demonstrate that democratic governments have authority to commit great injustices and severe harms—the kinds that would otherwise make the actor liable to be deceived, attacked, or killed.

THE COMPETENCE PRINCIPLE AS AN OBJECTION TO AUTHORITY

To review, one of the arguments for the special immunity thesis holds that governments enjoy special immunity *because* they have legitimacy and authority.[16] So far we've seen that legitimacy is irrelevant. What matters is whether governments have authority. Yet we've seen that even with this clarification, the assertion faces some big challenges. First, it's unclear that *any* governments have any authority, period. All the major arguments for government authority fail, and that gives us reason to think the "duty to obey the law" may be nothing more than a popular myth. Second, even if governments have some general authority—for example, the authority to make you pay taxes—a person who tries to ground the special immunity thesis on authority would need to show that governments specifically have the authority to commit *severe injustices* or impose serious harms.

In this section, I'll present a challenge to that claim—that is, to the claim that government agents have the specific authority to commit severe injustices or impose serious harms. This challenge won't cover every instance in which a government causes severe injustice or imposes serious harms, but it will cover a great number of them, and will cover most of the examples from the previous two chapters.

Suppose six criminal defendants are about to stand trial for first-degree murder. If they are found guilty, they will face many years or even life in prison, or perhaps even be executed. Imagine each jury suffers from some defect and then consider whether it seems justifiable to impose the jury's decision on the defendants.

> The first jury is *ignorant*. It does not pay attention to the details of the case and has no idea what the facts are. When it comes time to vote, the jurors flip a coin and find the defendant guilty.

> The second jury is *irrational*. It pays attention to the evidence, but processes that information in unreasonable and senseless ways. For instance, it interprets the evidence as showing that the defendant is actually an evil alien trying to conquer the world, and for that reason, finds him guilty.

> The third jury is *impaired*. It wants to give the defendant a fair trial, but some of the jurors are not smart enough to understand the evidence, while others cannot see or hear it. In the end, the jurors decide to find him guilty, even though none understood what the facts were.

> The fourth jury is *reckless*. It paid some attention to the facts and probably could have reached a fair decision had the jurors thought things through. But they were impatient to get to lunch and so quickly decided their defen-

dant was guilty without having thought things through with any degree of care.

The fifth jury is *prejudiced*. It decides to find the defendant guilty not because the evidence shows that he is but instead because he's black, and the jurors think all black people are scary and dangerous.

The sixth jury is *corrupt*. It finds the defendant guilty not because the evidence shows he is but rather because the jurors each received a bribe to do so.

Ask yourself: If we knew that the juries made their decisions that way, would we be obligated to obey them? (Would it be permissible to enforce their decisions, if we knew they had made their decisions that way?)

Intuitively, in each case, the decisions lack any sort of legitimacy or authority. If a defendant knew he had been subject to one of these juries, he would have no moral obligation to regard their decisions as authoritative.[17] That the jury found him guilty provides in itself no reason for him to accept punishment. (If he did in fact commit the crimes, he would have independent reasons for submitting to punishment.)

What explains these moral judgments? In a jury trial, the following features obtain:

1. The jury is charged with making a morally momentous decision, as it must decide how to apply principles of justice. It is the vehicle by which justice is to be delivered. It has special duties to administer justice.

2. The jury's decision can greatly affect the defendant's and others' life prospects. It can deprive the defendant of life, liberty, and/or property, or cause serious or lasting harm.

3. The jury is part of a system that claims sole jurisdiction to decide the case. That is, the system claims a monopoly on decision-making power, and expects the defendant and others to accept as well as abide by the decision.

4. The jury's decision will be imposed, involuntarily, by force or threats of force.

These seem to be good grounds for holding that juries have strong duties toward defendants or to the rest of us on whose behalf they act, and also that the jury's legitimacy and authority depends on its discharging these duties.[18]

The four features above are grounds for accepting what I call the *competence principle*:

People have a right that certain types of high-stakes decisions be made by competent people, who make their decisions competently and in good faith. It is unjust, and violates a person's rights, to forcibly deprive a citizen of life, liberty, or property, or significantly harm her life prospects, as a result of decisions made by an incompetent decision-making body, or decisions made incompetently or in bad faith. Political decisions are presumed legitimate and authoritative only when produced by competent political bodies in a competent way and good faith.

One justification for the competence principle is that it is unjust to expose people to undue risk. In the cases above, the jurists are acting negligently toward the defendant. From the defendant's point of view, a jury's decision is momentous, and the outcome is imposed involuntarily. In those kinds of cases, a jury has an obligation to take adequate care in making its decisions.

The competence principle appears to have a broad scope of application. There is little reason to think it applies only to juries. If a police officer, judge, politician, bureaucracy, or legislative body makes capricious, reckless, irrational, or malicious decisions, other people generally are stuck bearing high costs.[19] Government decisions tend to have these crucial features:

1. Governments are charged with making morally momentous decisions, as they must decide how to apply principles of justice and how to shape many of the basic institutions of society. They are one of the main vehicles through which justice is supposed to be established.

2. Government decisions tend to be of major significance. They can significantly harm citizen's life prospects, and deprive them of life, liberty, and property.

3. The government claims sole jurisdiction for making certain kinds of decisions over certain people within a geographic area. Governments expect people to accept and abide by their decisions.

4. The outcomes of decisions are imposed involuntarily through violence and threats of violence.

Individual government agents, branches, bureaucracies, and administrations, and the government as a whole, can also deprive citizens of life, liberty, and property. Like juries, they have the power to cause great harm. Like juries, they claim sole jurisdiction and the right to rule. Like juries, they impose their decisions on (potentially) innocent people who do not consent to these decisions. Like juries, they are charged with making, executing, and enforcing morally momentous decisions as well as deciding how to apply principles of justice.

Presumptively, just as defendants have a right not to be subject to incompetent jury trials, innocent people have a right not to be subject to badly made high-stakes political decisions. Presumptively, if the legitimacy and authority of jury decisions depend on competence and good faith, then so do the legitimacy and authority of all government decisions. If the legitimacy and authority of the jury system as whole depends on juries typically being reliable and acting in good faith, then we should say the same about other government branches, administrations, and practices.

The competence principle is, in itself, not a full theory of authority or legitimacy. Rather, as I'm arguing, it's a principle that should be part of a full theory, whatever the best theory of authority or legitimacy may be. Theories of legitimacy and authority are generally made up of two different kinds of principles. They have principles of disqualification—*disqualifiers*, for short—that articulate grounds *against* holding that certain regimes, people, bodies, decisions, or actions are authoritative or legitimate. They also have principles of qualification—*qualifiers*, for short—that articulate grounds on *behalf* of holding that certain regimes, people, bodies, or decisions are authoritative or legitimate.

The competence principle is a disqualifier. It does not justify imbuing anyone with power. It does not justify holding that any governments (or their agents) are authoritative or legitimate. Rather, it maintains that certain people, bodies, actions, or decisions *lack* authority and legitimacy, because either the people making the decisions are systematically incompetent, untrustworthy, and so on, or because the particular decision they made was made incompetently, maliciously, capriciously, or in bad faith.

The competence principle presents an additional challenge to the defender of the special immunity thesis. Consider again the following three cases, which I discussed previously:

A'. Minivan Shooter

Ann witnesses a police officer stop a minivan with a female driver and three children in the back. Ann sees that the driver has nothing in her hands and her hands are on the steering wheel. The police officer emerges from his car and starts shooting at the van's windows. Ann has a gun. She fires at the police officer before he shoots any of the children.

B'. Drunk Driver

Rodney, intoxicated after a night spent drinking, starts speeding on the highway. The cops try to pull him over. He ignores them, and then a high-speed chase ensues. When the cops finally pull him over, they do not merely yank him out of the car and arrest him. Rather, even after he is subdued and lying prostrate on the ground, they take turns clubbing him with their batons. Ann witnesses the beating and yells for them to stop. The cops ignore her. Finally, she pulls out her own weapon and fires at one of them in order to stop the beating as well as possibly save Rodney's life.

E'. Chief Executive Mastermind.

Walker is president. He initiates what is clearly an unjust war, though many people unreasonably believe it to be just. Under his command, the government kills tens of thousands of innocent civilians and soldiers in foreign countries. Thousands of domestic troops die in vain fighting Walker's wars. The war destroys massive amounts of property and wealth. Tens of thousands of civilians die from the war's fallout. Walker now plans to initiate another unjust war of the same sort in another country. Frank tries to use peaceful means to stop the war, but these fail. Frank intervenes. He kills Walker. As a result, this stops the next war, since Walker's successor is less belligerent.

In each of these cases, it's reasonable for Ann to believe not merely that what the wrongdoers are doing is unjust but that they are also acting incompetently or in bad faith. Police officers should know better than to shoot at minivans full of children. And so on.

When government agents act unjustly, they often act incompetently and in bad faith. In such cases, we have independent reasons (aside from the fact that the action is unjust) to hold that they lose whatever authority they might have had. Admittedly, however, the competence principle does not apply to every single instance of injustice. Consider again this case from the previous chapter:

G'. Regular Jailer

The district attorney, Bob, like many people in his town, believes that Ann might be a murderer. So one day, he gets the police to arrest Ann and holds a trial for her in the district court. Bob is a fanatic believer in due process so he makes sure Ann gets a proper trial. Ann is found guilty after a fair and proper trial. She is in fact innocent. As punishment, the jury decides that Ann will get life in prison. Ann's request for an appeal is turned down. At the first chance she gets, Ann makes a shiv, stabs a guard, and escapes.

In G', I specified that the trial was conducted competently and in good faith, even though it got the wrong answer. (Ann is in fact innocent, although the jury justifiably concluded that she was guilty beyond a reasonable doubt.)

The competence principle does not invalidate the government's authority (if it has any) in this case. Still, no philosopher has so far produced a good argument showing that governments have authority in cases like this.

DOES THIS TRIVIALIZE THE MORAL PARITY THESIS?

Many philosophers would say it's obvious why government agents (or at least democratic agents acting ex officio) enjoy special immunity. They say that special immunity follows from the fact that governments are legitimate and authoritative. Yet as we've seen, this seemingly obvious justification is full of problems. First, even if we grant that governments may legitimately do whatever they please, strictly speaking this leaves open what we may do in response. It leaves open that we may resist, evade, ignore, or defy them. All that could be relevant is whether governments have authority. Second, if we take seriously the past twenty-five hundred years of work on government authority, it's reasonable to think that no governments have authority in general. The problem is that all the arguments that philosophers have produced for government authority are defective, and we seem to have an identifiable psychological bias to believe authority exists even where there is none. Third, even if we ignore that and presume charitably that governments have some general kind of authority, in order to defend the special Immunity thesis, one would need to show specifically that governments have the authority to *commit severe injustices*—the very injustices against which we would be warranted in using defensive actions if a private civilian committed them. Fourth, the competence principle gives us reason to think many government injustices lack authority. At most, governments could be authoritative in committing a severe injustice only if they somehow decided to commit that injustice competently and in good faith.

One worry for me, though, is that if governments lack authority, then this threatens to trivialize my argument in this book. If governments lack authority, one might think that of course the special immunity thesis is false and the moral parity thesis is true. After all, isn't authority the best explanation for why governments would enjoy special immunity?

One response to that worry is to say I'm just exposing some of the largely unnoticed implications of the downfall of the doctrine of government authority: not only do we lack any duty to obey the law but wrongdoing government agents are also, like wrongdoing civilians, fair game for defensive violence, sabotage, and deception. Furthermore, as we'll see in future chapters, many of the extant major theories of civil disobedience presume that governments have the authority to commit severe injustice or at least a general kind of authority. But since governments probably lack *any* authority, let alone the authority to commit severe injustices, we need to revise our theories of civil disobedience. One of the goals in this book is to do that.

Contrary to the worry, however, even if governments lack authority, this doesn't trivialize my thesis here. As we'll see in the next chapter, there are a number of other seemingly plausible justifications for the special immunity thesis—justifications that do not rely on the assumption of government authority.

CHAPTER 4

Other General Arguments for Special Immunity

Let's look now at a range of general arguments for the special immunity thesis. Each of the arguments below tries to identify some special property P, which governments or their agents possess, and which is meant to show why they are due extra deference or enjoy special immunity. But as we'll see, each of these arguments fails.

ANTIVIGILANTISM

One might try to justify the special immunity thesis by claiming that using defensive actions against democratic officials is an instance of impermissible vigilante justice. As Estlund says, "Vigilante justice is commonly assumed to be wrong once there is an adequate public justice system." He adds, "When there is a system that serves the purposes of judgment and punishment without private punishment, then private punishment is morally wrong."[1]

The argument against vigilantism is familiar. John Locke contends that each of us has the right to punish rights violators in the state of nature. But he claims that we are biased judges, too lenient on ourselves and too harsh on those who harm us. Private punishment thus creates various "inconveniences," and our disagreements over private punishment could lead to conflict. Locke maintains that we should resolve this problem by instituting (as best we can) an impartial, public system of justice, which will correct those inconveniences and overcome our biases. Once that system is established, we should defer to it. We should alienate our private right to punish.[2]

Let's suppose here for the sake of argument, however, that there is indeed a strict moral prohibition against engaging in private punishment when there is a reasonably just and effective public system of punishment in play. Even if so, this assumption is irrelevant.

Invoking antivigilantism here seems to conflate using defensive actions against wrongdoers to stop them from harming others with punishment. Antivigilante arguments are supposed to show that under certain conditions, private citizens must transfer their so-called natural right to punish to the state. Yet the question of permissible defensive action is not about the right to punish. None of the cases A–M or A'–M' from chapter 2 involve defender Ann punishing anyone. If I claim Ann may stop the hawkish president, I do not claim she has the right to *punish* him. Instead, I am just saying that she may attack him to stop him from killing innocent people. If I claim (as I will argue at length in chapter 6) that a politician may lie to bad voters to prevent them from electing a bad candidate, I am not claiming that the politician may therefore punish the voters. So it looks like a moral prohibition against vigilante punishment is irrelevant.

Still, one could just amend the antivigilantism objection by saying that we have a moral obligation to allow *government officials* to administer justice, protect others, and so on. We should not try to do these things ourselves; we should let the police take care of it.

But even with this improvement, the antivigilantism objection doesn't justify the special immunity thesis. The problem is that the principle does not offer us any grounds for distinguishing between cases A–M and A'–M'. The antivigilante principle forbids us from taking justice into our own hands. It tells us we must instead let the government take care of problems. This reasoning, though, applies equally well to *Shooter in the Park* as it does to *Minivan Shooter*. In both cases, Ann is a "vigilante": she stops the wrongdoers herself rather than waiting for the police to stop the wrongdoers. So if the antivigilante principle explains why we must not use defensive action against the democratic officials in A'–M', it seems also to imply that we cannot use defensive action against the civilians in A–M.

What the defender of the special immunity thesis needs is some version of the antivigilante principle that allows defensive action in A–M but not A'–M'. Otherwise, she's not arguing for special immunity but rather for moral parity, while simultaneously rejecting commonsense moral principles about defensive action.

On this point, if the antivigilante principle always forbids violence, even in cases A–M, then the principle seems implausible. When there is an indeed an effective and impartial method for administering justice, perhaps one should tend to defer to that system. Yet in each of the A–M cases, Ann is in an emergency situation. In these situations, waiting for the government to fix the problem means innocent people suffer, period. When governments are more effective at taking care of the problem and are actually doing so (or could easily be induced to do so), then the antivigilante principle is plausible. In those cases, perhaps citizens should let the state handle the problem. If those conditions are not met, however, then there's no obvious reason to hold that citizens must defer to the state.

Suppose I witness a man trying to rape a woman. There are police nearby. I implore them to intervene. They respond, "Sorry, we're on break. Check back with us later." I call 911. The operator says, "All of our officers are busy. We can be there in forty-five minutes." If the antivigilante principle claims that even then, I may not defend the woman, the principle seem absurd. It certainly conflicts with the commonsense moral principles captured in common law.

Or suppose Bane has captured Gotham City. Now suppose Batman has a plan for defeating Bane—one that has a good chance of success, while the government's plan is far worse. In that case, rather than saying that Batman should defer to the government, the government should defer to Batman. What could the government's argument be otherwise? "Hey, Batman, we know that you are more likely to save Gotham than we are, but we care far more about being in charge than we do about actually seeing lives saved and justice done. We demand you step aside."

So it seems that citizens have no obligation to defer to government when government cannot solve the problem as well as they can or when it simply will not solve the problem. In real life, of course, it would rarely be the case that a lone vigilante would do a better job defeating terrorists than a well-organized government. In many cases, civilians should thus defer. Still, in cases like A–M or A'–M', Ann, who is in the right place at the right time, is better positioned to protect the innocent than any government agents are.

PEACEFUL ALTERNATIVES

Consider the following argument:

> Democracies provide peaceful and effective avenues for citizens to remove unjust leaders and bring unjust leaders to justice. There are peaceful and effective legal procedures

for citizens to stop their governments from committing injustice. Citizens should use these procedures instead of using violence against their leaders or government agents.

This might seem like an objection to the moral parity thesis and argument in support of the special immunity thesis. But it's not.

Rather, it's at most an elaboration of the necessity proviso on permissible defensive actions. Recall, for instance, that according to both McMahan's theory of permissible killing and the common law, defensive killing is permissible only when it's reasonably believed necessary to protect oneself or others from a grave threat. If a nonlethal alternative is known to be just as effective in preventing that threat, we may not kill the wrongdoers. But this point applies just as much to killing civilians as it does to killing democratic officials. Similar points apply to other, nonlethal forms of defensive action.

As an empirical generalization, it might be that we are more likely to have peaceful means of stopping democratic government's wrongdoing than we have to halt acts of civilian wrongdoing. If so, it might be, also as an empirical generalization, that the conditions under which it is permissible to kill a wrongdoer are less likely to obtain when the wrongdoer is a government agent than when he's a private civilian. But this remains compatible with the moral parity thesis because it allows that the conditions under which it is permissible to kill wrongdoers are the same.

Here we nevertheless need to distinguish between *patterns* of wrongdoing versus individual acts of wrongdoing. Consider the following two problems:

1. Police in a particular city have a well-deserved reputation for corruption and abuse. There's lots of evidence that

they take advantage of prostitutes, abuse and mistreat minorities, shake down people for money, and so on. Further, when Internal Affairs investigates them, they have a tendency to lie or keep quiet; they're more concerned with protecting their comrades in blue than they are with promoting justice.

2. Ann witnesses the equivalent of the Rodney King beating.

Violent resistance may be effective in stopping the problem in the second case; it will rarely be effective in helping with the problems described in the first one. If Ann shoots the police office in the second situation, it's not as though she's trying to "fix" the police. Rather, she's trying to save a life, and her actions are justifiable by the commonsense doctrine of the defense of others. But if she wants to solve the deeper pattern of abuse, shooting individual cops as they commit severe injustices is unlikely to help. She'll instead probably need to pursue peaceful means of reform.

Consider these two cases again:

C. Health Nut
Health guru John sincerely believes that caffeine is unhealthy, causes laziness, and induces people to use hard drugs. John announces that in order to protect his neighbors and promote the social good, he and his followers will capture coffee drinkers, confiscate their belongings, and imprison them in John's filthy basement for years. Ann, who is too poor to move away from town, loves coffee. She secretly drinks it in the morning in her kitchen. One day, a henchman breaks into her house and attempts to capture her. She struggles to defend herself, and in the process, kills him.

C'. War on Drugs

Town leaders decide to make marijuana illegal, even though there is overwhelming evidence that marijuana is in every respect less harmful than alcohol—a drug that is legal for any adult to consume. Ann has a pot stash in her house. One night, a bunch of police officers raid Ann's house in a no-knock raid. She recognizes that they are police officers. She also knows that if they capture her, she will be imprisoned for a decade. Her government issues overly punitive sentences for drug possession and is unresponsive to citizens' demands to overturn the law. Ann resists arrest and escapes.

There is an important empirical difference between these two cases. It is far more likely that organized, peaceful political activity will succeed in overturning marijuana criminalization laws in case C' than such activity will succeed in getting John to change his mind in case C. Democratic governments have built-in mechanisms that make them somewhat responsive to citizens' demands. Indeed, as I've been writing this book, more and more states have decriminalized marijuana, and the federal government has largely backed off enforcing its marijuana laws in those states. (The federal government still criminalizes marijuana, and strictly speaking, the states lack the legal authority to overturn federal laws within their state borders.)

Still, it's unclear what bearing any of this has on what Ann may do in either C or C'. Remember, this book is concerned specifically with *defensive action* people may undertake to protect themselves from injustice. I'm not here asking about the related but distinct question of what kinds of activities people may or may not undertake to change the law. Assume marijuana and caffeine criminalization are unjust. (That should be an easy assumption.) The question of whether you may violently resist arrest and incarceration for consuming these substances is not the same as the question of whether you may use violence, subterfuge, and so on to change the law. Consider these three examples of behavior:

1. A police officer tries to arrest Ann for marijuana possession. Ann punches him in the head, knocking him unconscious, and walks way.

2. Ann works as a police officer. She often encounters people in possession of pot. Even though the law tells her to arrest them, she ignores that law and never arrests them for it.

3. Ann shows up at the Drug Enforcement Administration with a bomb and demands that it remove marijuana from the controlled substances list.

The third case is importantly different from the first two, which are about resisting or refusing to comply with a bad law. The third case is about trying to use violence to *change* a bad law. Here, I'm only concerned with the first two cases.

I think it's probably true that in general, violence is a bad way to produce social change. That said, the question of when and to what extent violence works is a rather nuanced *empirical* one. For instance, two recent books, Charles Cobb Jr.'s *This Non-Violent Stuff'll Get You Killed* and Akinyele Omowale Umoja's *We Will Shoot Back* make convincing cases that violent resistance to individual acts of injustice were *essential* to helping the nonviolent part of the black civil rights movement succeed (as much as it has). According to Umoja, the later "nonviolent" phase of activism worked only because in earlier phases, blacks had armed themselves and shot back in self-defense. Whites initially responded to black activism by beating, killing, and lynching blacks. Armed blacked militias fought back, sometimes by killing cops or national guard members. Once whites learned that blacks would fight back, they turned to less violent forms of oppression, and blacks in turn began using the nonviolent tactics with which we are familiar. But this nonviolent phase would have been impossible had blacks not violently defended themselves.

Still, all this has little bearing on what Ann may do in case C'. In case C', Ann has no plausible peaceful way of avoiding having her rights seriously violated. Even if she is found innocent, she is still likely to have to spend a significant amount of time unjustly imprisoned and significant amount of money fighting against an injustice.

Consider these variations of C and C': suppose Ann has strong reason to believe that if she goes to trial for marijuana possession, she will eventually be found not guilty. Yet suppose that she would still have to spend thirty days in jail and $10,000 in legal fees. Now suppose she had identical circumstances with regard to John the Jailer. Suppose she had equally strong reasons to think that John's private jury will find her not guilty of caffeine possession, but she will have to spend thirty days in John's private jail and $10,000 in legal fees. In both cases, she has equally good "peaceful means" to avoid the injustice of even further harm, but in both cases, she has to unjustly endure thirty days in jail and lose $10,000. If you are inclined to treat these cases differently, it doesn't look like the peaceful means issue is doing the work for you.

GOOD FAITH AND FOLLOWING ORDERS

One might argue that a key difference between the civilian (A–M) and government agent (A'–M') cases has to do with the wrongdoers' intentions. In *Terrorist*, Cobra Commander has evil motivations. In *Hawk*, we might presume that the president tries in good faith to serve the nation's interests; he just has horrible ideas about how to do so. The argument is that because the government agents are acting in good faith, trying to serve the common good, using the powers granted to them specifically for that purpose, then they enjoy special immunity against defensive actions.

To begin with, note if this argument succeeds at all in justifying special immunity, it does so only when government agents in fact have good intentions. It would still allow that it is permissible to use defensive actions against government agents, acting ex officio, provided they were not acting in good faith. Many times government agents do not in fact act in good faith or have bad intentions. (They of course have every incentive to pretend that they are always well motivated.)

Beyond that, the argument has the same fatal flaws as the previous two. It fails to offer an interesting difference between cases involving civilians and government agents. Suppose for the sake of argument that using defensive action against a wrongdoer is permissible only if the wrongdoer has bad intentions. Even if so, civilian wrongdoers also sometimes have good intentions. In case C, *Health Nut*, the wrongdoers intend to *help* people. They believe that caffeine is disastrously bad for everyone.

The good faith objection doesn't therefore show that the conditions under which it is permissible to defend against government agents are more stringent than those under which it is permissible to defend against civilians. Rather, at most it allows that the conditions are the same. It then leaves it open, as an empirical question, whether any particular wrongdoing agent, governmental or civilian, "means well" when she acts badly. So this good faith objection, if sound at all, is compatible with the moral parity thesis and does not support the special immunity thesis.

Most philosophers who have written about the morality of killing think that acting in good faith does make a moral difference. The moral principles that govern killing a well-intentioned agent who acts in good faith, but who makes a moral error, are different than those that govern the killing of a badly intentioned agent. So, for instance, suppose we modify *Shooter in the Park* somewhat. Imagine there are five badly intentioned shooters and only one child. It seems justifiable to kill all five of them to save the one child. We don't have to weigh one life against five, because the shooters are culpable while the child is innocent.

In contrast, suppose there are five gunmen and only one child, but suppose they have *good* intentions. Suppose the gunmen sincerely believe the child is infected with a zombie apocalypse virus, as in *28 Days Later* or *I Am Legend*. Suppose the gunmen have had such a bizarre set of experiences that their belief is justified though false. The gunmen justifiably but falsely believe that the child will soon turn into a zombie and that killing the child is necessary to save the world from a zombie apocalypse. Suppose Ann *knows* this about the gunmen: she knows that they *mean well*. In this case, one might think that the gunmen are "innocent aggressors" and saving the child's life must be balanced against saving theirs.[3]

That seems plausible, though one might plausibly disagree and think that innocent aggressors are liable to be killed. It's an interesting intramural debate and one of the hard cases for the theory of defensive violence. As far as I can tell, the dominant view is that innocent aggressors are liable to defensive action, but not as liable as culpable aggressors.

But we don't have to settle that debate here. Again, at most this would show that there is a statistical difference between government agents and civilian actors. It might turn out empirically that when government agents and private civilians commit the same injustices, the former are more likely than the latter to be innocent aggressors acting in good faith. This still allows that the moral principles governing killing them are the same, though. Government agents do not enjoy special immunity; rather, a small subset of well-motivated agents might qualify as innocent aggressors.

A closely related argument holds that the key difference between many civilian and governmental wrongdoers is that the latter are, at least in many cases, just following orders. This explains why the former are liable to be killed when the latter are not. On closer inspection, however, this cannot explain the difference in liability between the two.

After all, civilian wrongdoers who are liable to be killed might be following orders. Suppose a criminal kingpin orders his goons to kill Frank's family. Frank is justified in killing the goons in defense of others. Or in case C, *Health Nut*, Ann is justified in killing the henchman, even though the henchman is following orders.

What matters here isn't whether the civilian or governmental agent is following orders but instead whether the orders are *just*. If a lieutenant orders soldiers to massacre the residents of My Lai, anyone could still justifiably kill the soldiers to stop the massacre. On the other hand, if a police captain orders his officers to arrest a murderer, the murderer should not resist because the murderer should in fact be arrested and tried.

One might finally try to say that "following orders" makes a difference because those who follow the orders are sometimes under threat of duress. For instance, a soldier or cop who fails to follow an unjust order might suffer a penalty, including, in some situations, execution. As McMahan concludes, a person who is a threat to others but is acting under duress to some extent might be an "Excused Threat."[4] The idea here is that acting under duress partly relieves a person of his culpability in doing the wrongful action. As McMahan argues, excused threats are still liable to be killed under the same conditions as unexcused threats.

To see why, consider case A, *Shooter in the Park*, again. Suppose Ann learned that the only reason the shooter was shooting the children was because a criminal had threatened to hurt the shooters' son unless he in turn killed ten other innocent children. Here the shooter might not be completely blameworthy for trying to kill the children in the park, but Ann is still justified in shooting him in order to protect them. So it also goes with governmental cases. Suppose a democratic government conscripts soldiers and orders them, on pain of execution, to invade a country and kill its innocent citizens as well as soldiers. The innocent citizens and soldiers of the invaded country— or you, or I—may still kill the invading soldiers, though many of the soldiers qualify as excused threats.

Again, one might reasonably dispute that and hold that we have to balance the lives of excused threats against their potential victims. And there could be similar debates regarding other forms of defensive actions against excused threats.

But regardless of what the truth is here, this does not in principle provide a difference between government and civilian wrongdoers or threats. It's possible that, as a matter of fact, government agents tend to be more likely to be excused threats than civilians. Nevertheless, that's compatible with the moral parity thesis, as it allows that both are rightful subjects of defensive action under the same conditions.

IS BELIEF IN MORAL PARITY DANGEROUS?

What I call the dangerous misapplication objection goes as follows:

> We are poor judges of consequences. We are prone to vengeance and anger. If this book's position on assassination were widely believed, people would probably misapply the principles in dangerous ways. In any real-life scenario, if a person believes himself permitted to attack a congressperson or president, he should recognize he is prone to error, and should be extremely skeptical of his conclusion that assassination is permitted in this instance.

In effect, this objection says that my argument is self-effacing. That is, if people believed it, they would misapply it. While trying to conform to my position on defensive action, they would act in ways not actually authorized by this position.

This objection is closely related to a mistaken objection people sometimes raise against the view that people may break unjust laws. Recall in chapter 3 that I discussed how it's unclear whether governments have any authority at all, let alone the specific authority to issue unjust laws, rules, edicts, and commands. I was talking about this point with a law professor a few years ago, when the professor asked, "So you think people may break unjust laws?"

"Sure," I responded. "And indeed I hope they do and that they get away with it."

"But surely you can't mean that a person can break any law just because he thinks it's unjust. That's a license for anarchy!"

"Right, I don't mean that," I replied. "But notice the difference between what you said and what I said. I'm saying that some laws are in fact unjust—that there's an independent moral truth about whether laws are just or not. When the law is in fact unjust, then there is no duty to obey it. That's not the same thing as saying that you can break any law because you *believe* it's unjust."

"But might someone be mistaken? Don't they have to judge for themselves?" he asked.

"Of course," I said. "But that's a problem for *every* theory. Every moral theory says something like, 'Under conditions A, you must do X; under conditions B, you must not do Y; and so on.' The theories don't say 'Do X when you simply *judge* you're in A'; after all, you might be mistaken, negligent, or reckless in making that judgment. Instead, they say, 'Do X when you are *in fact* in A.' Notice the difference."

In short, the general theory of defensive action says that we can use defensive actions under certain conditions. Call those conditions C for short. As we saw in chapter 2, among those conditions is that a defensive actor must reasonably believe that defensive action is warranted. Some might disagree and think the epistemic conditions are more stringent: the defensive actor must be *justified* in her belief or must have only a low chance of being mistaken. We don't need to decide that debate here.

The moral parity thesis says conditions C are also sufficient for using defensive action against government agents acting ex officio. The special immunity thesis denies that, asserting that defensive action is permissible against government agents under a much more tightly constrained set of conditions or not at all.

The dangerous misapplication objection fails for the same reason self-effacing objections usually do in general. The fact that most people would botch applying a theory does not show that the theory is wrong.

So, for instance, suppose—as is frequently argued—that most people would misapply utilitarian moral standards. Utilitarian moral theories all claim that what makes actions right or wrong is in some ways a function of their actual or expected consequences. But as many critics claim, applying utilitarianism is too hard for the common person, in part because most people don't know enough to determine what the likely consequences of their actions will be.

Even if so, this does not invalidate utilitarianism. Even if everyone consistently misapplied utilitarianism, this would not show the theory is false.[5] As David Brink notes, utilitarian moral theory means to provide a *criterion of right*, not a *method for making decisions*.[6] The difference is as follows:

- *Criterion/Criteria of Right: A principle or set of principles that explains which features make actions right, wrong, supererogatory, required, permitted but not required, or forbidden.*
- *Decision Procedure / Method for Making Decisions: A set of principles, questions, thought experiments, vi-*

sualization techniques, breathing exercises, physical ex-
ercises, or whatnot that when followed, help the moral
agent do whatever is morally required.

These are two different things. Utilitarianism is supposed to explain what makes actions right and wrong. Whether it is useful—given flawed human psychology—as an algorithm or tool for people on the ground to make decisions is a different matter. It might turn out that utilitarianism is the right moral theory. But if we want to give people help on the ground in doing what's right and wrong, it may also turn out that the best method isn't to have them think about philosophical issues but instead perhaps imagine their parents are watching them or they will have to later explain their actions to others. Or perhaps people should use rules of thumb. Or perhaps, if they're hotheaded, the best method is to count to ten and then go with their guts. Or perhaps, if they're George Costanza from the TV show *Seinfeld*, the best decision method is to do the *opposite* of whatever their intuition tells them. The criteria of right action are the same for us all, but the best decision procedure might vary from person to person given the peculiarities of our individual psychology.

Many utilitarians, such as Mill, thus think that while utilitarianism tells us what actually makes actions right and wrong, the typical layperson should just follow a set of basic moral rules (e.g., don't steal or kill) rather than try to calculate the consequences of various actions. Utilitarianism identifies what makes actions right or wrong, but for most people, it does not offer a useful decision procedure for determining what is right and wrong. The math is too hard.

If that seems weird, consider as an analogy how baseball works. Certain physics equations explain why the baseball lands where it does. These physics equations capture the truth of the matter. Yet most outfielders would never catch a ball if they tried to do so by "applying" the equations. Unless they are math wizards, doing so is too hard and slow. So the decision procedure that they should use on the ground for catching the ball is whatever psychological and physical mechanisms are most likely to get the ball. The equations explain the ball's path, but do not provide a decision procedure for catching balls.

Lying, deception, sabotage, destruction, and violence are dangerous. We should be self-aware and recognize that we are prone to error. We should be aware that defensive actions are morally risky. We should also be aware of our own epistemic uncertainty.

Suppose Ann comes across what appears to be a police officer about to execute someone. Should she shoot him to stop him? One might argue no for the following reasons:

> It's strange for police officers to just try to murder innocent people. Though it *seems* like that's what the police officer is doing, Ann should give the officer the benefit of the doubt and presume that there must be some good reason he's doing what he's doing. She should thus not kill him, at least not until she's more certain or has more information.

This new objection—let's call it the epistemic uncertainty objection—gets something right. On reflection, however, it doesn't do the work that defenders of the special immunity thesis need it to do.

Recall that one of the conditions for defensive violence was that the defender had to have a *reasonable* belief that the defensive action was necessary to prevent the purported aggressor from committing a severe injustice or harm. As I discussed, we can reasonably debate just how much epistemic justification is required for a belief to be reasonable or what beliefs are reasonable in different situations. This doesn't mean the question is highly controversial. Some beliefs are obviously reasonable, some are obviously not, and others are in the middle area of, well, reasonable debate about what's reasonable. Putting all that aside, the point remains that so long as the defender's belief is sufficient epistemic warrant and the other conditions for defensive action are met, then defensive action is permissible. The defender does not need to be certain.

Now there's an interesting question here about what we should infer when we see government agents doing something that appears to be unjust. While there is rampant police abuse in the United States, it would be absurd for me to take action as soon as a police officer pulls someone over who appears to be a drunk driver. Let's say the driver is white. Most likely the officer will not use excessive force or violence against the drunk driver but instead act in a professional and diligent manner. On the other hand, if I see him immediately drag the driver out, knock him down, and then start pummeling the driver with the barrel of his gun, then while it's possible the officer *had* to do that to protect himself, most likely he's engaging in excessive violence and is a rightful target of defensive action himself.

In some cases, we have reasons to presume that what the government is doing is unjust even if we lack other details. For instance, since we have evidence that drone strikes kill an unacceptably high percentage and number of civilians, we might feel free to shoot down any drone we see.[7]

In the end, these points do not illustrate a particularly interesting difference between government and nongovernmental agents. At most, the point here is that when we form beliefs about what others are doing, we have to rely on statistical trends and background information. It's possible that we might encounter situations in which two people seem to be doing the same thing—something that looks potentially unjust, but based on our background knowledge about those people or people like them, we might infer that more likely one of them has a justification for what she's doing and the other doesn't. Suppose I turn the corner and see a police officer beating someone with a baton. Suppose in another scenario, I turn the corner and see an ordinary man beating another man with a bat. Now it's statistically more likely that cases like second one are instances of injustice than are cases like the first; it's more likely that a police officer beating a person is justified in doing so than is a random person. A person considering defensive action has to take into account these sorts of things when forming beliefs about whether defensive action is necessary. But in the end, all this shows at most is that in some cases, government agents who *seem* like they might be doing something unjust are less likely to actually be doing something unjust than civilians doing the same thing. All this is compatible with the moral parity thesis and allows that we may use defensive actions in cases like A'–M'.

In summary, in the real world, when we think defensive violence or other defensive actions are justified (according to the argument presented here), we should be extra cautious and self-skeptical. But none of this shows that defensive actions are always forbidden or government agents should enjoy special immunity against defensive action.

All that being said, I wonder if this objection mostly has the problem backward. The worry here is supposed to be an epistemic problem: that people will *misapply* the theory, mistakenly resisting government agents even when they should not. On the contrary, it seems more plausible that citizens are more likely to engage in wrongful obedience than they are to engage in wrongful resistance. The typical person is a conformist, deferential to authority, and fearful for their own safety. When they watch cops beating a person to death, they don't intervene; they film it and put it on YouTube. When their governments order them to kill foreigners in an unjust war, they do.

Consider the Milgram experiment.[8] This experiment seemingly shows that we will obey orders even when we believe what we are being ordered to do (deliver seemingly life-threatening shocks to a fellow experimental subject) is immoral and we want to disobey. We respond to social pressure by *caving in* and becoming cowards.

During the experiment, Stanley Milgram brought in two "subjects"—one of whom was secretly an actor. He assigned the role of a teacher to the real subject, and gave the actor the role of a learner, and then told them they were taking part in an experiment on memory. The teacher was told to ask the learner a question. If the learner made a mistake, the teacher was to punish him by delivering an electric shock. (The apparent shocks went up in fifteen-volt increments, and also had labels such as "danger: intense shock" and "XXX" at the extreme end.)

The teacher, after observing the learner being handcuffed to a chair and hooked up to electrodes, was taken to another room and told to begin the test. The learner/actor began giving incorrect answers according to a script. In some versions of the experiment, the learner would scream or else complain about his heart condition. In all versions, the learner would eventually stop answering the questions altogether. For all that the teacher knew, the learner had passed out or died. If at any point the teacher expressed concern or said he wanted to stop, a lab director, following a script, would tell the teacher, "The experiment requires you to continue" or "please continue." The lab director also ordered the teacher to treat nonresponses as incorrect answers and deliver a higher shock.

In most versions of the experiment, almost all the teachers agreed to administer high-level shocks, despite showing clear and obvious discomfort over the fact that they were torturing another human being. Once the learner stopped responding, 65 percent of the subjects/teachers kept going, sending for all they knew what were increasingly lethal shocks into a possibly unconscious or dead fellow subject.[9]

Most subjects showed obvious discomfort with what they were doing. Some laughed or cried; some became hysterical. Many asked the lab director *who was responsible*; the lab director would quietly assure them that *he* was. Only a minority *quit* and refused to deliver the highest-voltage shock. During the debriefing afterward, Milgram or his director asked subjects why they didn't stop. Many subjects showed surprise, as if it hadn't occurred to them that they could just *stop*.

This is just one major experiment, of course. But in general, it seems that psychology shows that citizens tend to err on the side of wrongful obedience rather than the side of wrongful resistance. From the Milgram experiments to contemporary work on intergroup bias in political psychology, we see that citizens are generally conformists who do what they are told and try to avoid conflict.[10]

What if we go outside the laboratory? Consider the My Lai massacre, Nazi concentration camps, Soviet gulags, Holodomor, Armenian Genocide, Yangzhou massacre, and other such atrocities. In each case, higher-level officials order lower-level agents or even civilians to commit atrocities, and they overwhelming agree to do so, even when they have the power to refuse.

Thus, to whatever extent the dangerous misapplication and epistemic uncertainty objections push against my view, they push even harder against the other side. If anything, proponents of the special immunity thesis should be cautious in expounding their views. People are far more likely to support and obey a Hitler or Stalin than they are to stand up to a police officer when they should back down.

RETALIATION, FALLOUT, AND EXTORTION

We are still looking for reasons why it would be impermissible to engage in defensive actions against government officials in cases A'–M' even though it is permissible to engage in defensive actions against civilians in the analogous cases A–M. One such objection goes as follows:

The Fallout Objection
If citizens believed they were at liberty to resist democratic officials (under the principles described above), then this would cause dangerous instability and fallout. If civilians resist a bad cop, the other cops are likely to retaliate by harming other innocent people or curbing their rights. If civilians attack an evil president, future presidents and Congress are likely to retaliate by harming other people or further violating their rights. Therefore, it is wrong to take defensive action against democratic officials.

The idea here is that morality is a strategic game. What I am permitted to do might depend on how others will respond to what I do. Perhaps what would otherwise have been a permissible action might be rendered impermissible if others will perform wrongful actions in response to it. That is, perhaps the threat of extortion might change my moral duties.

Consider, as an example, that there's no moral duty to choose a red over a blue toothbrush. Suppose, though, that a terrorist threatens to nuke Washington, DC, unless I choose blue. Must I then choose blue? By virtue of the terrorist issuing a threat, do I come to acquire a duty to comply?

Consider a variation on the *Minivan Shooter* (case A'). Suppose Ann is about to stop the cop who is shooting at the children. But just as she does so, the cop yells to her, "We cops stick together. If you shoot me, my buddies in blue will retaliate and kill *other* kids. That's not a threat; that's a promise." Suppose his threat is credible. Is it still permissible for Ann to save the kids or must she back down?

Or suppose a woman is about to be raped. She fights back violently. Yet as she does so, she hears the rapist's friend yell, "If you don't let him rape you, I promise to rape and murder three more women." Suppose the threat is credible. Is she required to submit to being raped?

Perhaps these are hard questions or questions with controversial answers. How we are required to respond to extortion is bound to be controversial.

For the sake of argument, suppose it is impermissible for you to use defensive action against a wrongdoer if there is a serious threat that the wrongdoer or others will respond by committing even greater harms or injustices. But notice that this does not merely show that certain government agents are immune to defensive action. It also demonstrates that many criminals and well-organized wrongdoers are immune to defensive action. After all, civilians can and often do respond to what otherwise would have been justifiable violent self-defense or the defense of others by threatening to cause even more harm. A bully on the playground might threaten to beat up two other kids if you stick up for your friend. The mafia can and does tell people that it'll hurt and kill even more people if its victims start to defend themselves. The Joker might threaten to bomb Gotham City if Batman tries to rescue Commissioner Gordon.

It may turn out, empirically, that democratic governments, or governments in general, are unusually willing and able to use extortion to prevent us from defending ourselves against their wrongdoing agents. If so, it may thus turn out, empirically, that the conditions under which it is permissible to resist a wrongdoer are less likely to obtain when the wrongdoer is a government agent than when he's a private civilian. But this remains compatible with the moral parity thesis because it allows that the conditions under which it is permissible to defend against wrongdoers are the same. In both cases, the fallout objection holds that we're allowed to resist wrongdoers in certain conditions—one of those conditions being that using defensive actions against the wrongdoers won't incite them or other wrongdoers to commit even greater harm or injustice. Again, all the fallout objection really does is suggest that the conditions under which it's permissible to use defensive actions against government agents, though they are the *same* as those for civilians, obtain less frequently than the do for civilians.

Note another peculiar feature of the fallout objection. It seems to suggest that using defensive action is *more* likely to be justifiable against democratic governments than against nondemocratic ones or organized criminal syndicates. Many people believe it is justifiable to assassinate totalitarian dictators, such as Stalin or Hitler. Killing a totalitarian dictator or criminal mastermind, however, seems more likely to endanger innocent third parties than killing a democratic official. Fanni Kaplan tried but failed to assassinate Vladimir Lenin in 1918. Lenin and his government responded with the Red Terror. Even if Kaplan had killed Lenin, there was a good chance Lenin would have been succeeded by someone worse or at least equally bad. (In fact, he was.) Totalitarian Communist regimes do not value individual human life. After a successful assassination, newly installed dictators are likely to terrorize citizens into submission. Similar remarks apply to, say, the mafia. If a person stands up for himself against the mafia, the mafia is likely to respond by terrorizing everyone into submission.

Compare this to the United States and other democracies. Four US presidents have been assassinated, and many more have been targets. Thirteen congresspersons have been assassinated, and a few others have been targets. Note, carefully, that I am not saying that any of these people were rightful targets of defensive action according to my theory. I invoke these cases to note the consequences: none of these events resulted in humanitarian disasters or terror purges.

Compared to other forms of government, democracies tend to be more concerned with their citizens' welfare. For this reason, democracies do not respond by crushing their citizens. Political scientists who study this issue empirically tend to find that fallout from assassination is minor.[11] Similar remarks likely apply to other forms of defensive action, though admittedly I could find no empirical work testing this hypothesis.

So far I have assumed for the sake of argument that we are required to surrender or submit to credible threats of extortion. But that's not obviously true, and I don't in general find the claim plausible. It is not obvious that what would have been a permissible action becomes wrong just because someone else threatens or is likely to threaten to react badly to it.

Let's return to the example from the last chapter, in which the United States holds a referendum on whether it should nuke Tuvalu. Again, suppose everyone in the United States except for me votes on behalf of nuking Tuvalu, but suppose I am justified in believing it has no good grounds for doing so. Suppose I assassinate the would-be Tuvalu-nuking president and his generals, even though I know my fellow citizens will react by rioting. During the riots, they would injure ten thousand innocent Americans (more than the population of Tuvalu). It's at least not obvious that this makes the assassination wrong when it otherwise would have been right. After all, my fellow citizens are obligated not to riot in response to my action, so that moral burden for that falls on them.

Act utilitarians—those who think the rightness and wrongness of an action is solely a function of the act's expected consequences—will of course hold that when deciding what to do, we must act strategically and make decisions based on what we expect others to do in response. If waving my hand right now would cause a vase to fall over and kill someone, I shouldn't do it. If waving my hand right now would incite a psychopath to smash someone's head with a vase, I shouldn't do it. From the act utilitarian perspective, these actions are the same. For a utilitarian, how *others* will react to our actions is just another feature of the world that we must consider when calculating the consequences and thus permissibility of our actions. But many of us view this as a bug rather than a feature of act utilitarianism, even if we might agree with act utilitarians in at least *some* such cases.

As Hurd says,

> Rights theorists—at least those who cash out the value of rights in terms of the liberty they purchase—ought to be deeply concerned by the claim that the liberty to exercise one's rights is rightly circumscribed by others' wrongs. While such a claim does not imply a conflict of rights of any traditional sort, it is perversely paradoxical. It implies that wrongdoers, by their wrongdoing, acquire rights that others should abandon actions that they (otherwise) have rights to do. While one does not have a right to do what others have rights that one not do, one acquires a right that others abandon their rights when one does what one has no right to do. In short, the perpetration of a wrong trumps the exercise of a right. Thus, while rights do not conflict, they shrink. Such a thesis surely offends intuitions that the justifiable uses of one's time, labor, and property ought not to be thought relative to the unjustifiable uses to which those resources might foreseeably be put by slubberdegullions and shirkers.[12]

Perhaps this is stated too strongly; it might not quite be that wrongdoers acquire rights that others abandon actions they have the rights to do. (Perhaps instead, the idea is that the would-be wrongdoer's potential victims have a right against us that we not defend ourselves or others.)[13] But the view does hold that we can lose our rights to defend ourselves or others, or that these rights can be quickly overridden, because other people might react badly. There's something rather perverse about that. It implies that whether you have (all things considered) a right to defend yourself or other people (including your loved ones) depends in part on whether the aggressor you defend yourself or others against can issue a credible threat. To return to a previous illustration, this view says that a woman can defend herself from being raped only if the rapist will not respond by hurting more people. The view implies that would-be war criminals, assailants, muggers, rapists, and murderers can—almost magically— make it impermissible to resist just by credibly promising that if anyone tries to stop them from hurting people, then they or their friends will hurt even more people.

To be clear, though, one does not have to be a utilitarian to hold that the right of self-defense or the defense of others vanishes when the attacker makes a credible threat. A nonutilitarian could agree to this position as well.

Now Hurd and I agree that at least in some cases, one does indeed acquire a duty to act differently because of other people's wrongdoing. At least in some cases, acts that would normally be permissible could become impermissible because others plan to act badly. Let's consider a few.

Suppose I work for Dick's Sporting Goods. An angry man comes in and loudly yells, "I caught my wife cheating on me with the neighbor. I'm going to beat them both up. Where are your baseball bats?" While normally it is permissible to sell people baseball bats, no questions asked, in this case I should not.

Similarly, suppose my intoxicated friend asks to borrow my keys so that he can go for a quick drive. Again, while normally it is permissible to let my friend drive my car, it's not permissible to do so when he is clearly drunk.[14]

In these two instances, by selling the bat or handing over the keys, I facilitate someone else in committing a wrong. Refusing to help them, by refusing to sell the bat or hand over the keys, imposes little or no harm on me.

Note, however, that these seem different from cases in which they *threaten* to do wrong if I don't help them. Suppose the man says, "If you don't give me a bat, I'm going to beat up my wife." Or suppose my friend says, "If you don't let me borrow your car, I promise to get drunk and then drive around town in someone else's car until I hit someone." In these situations, by refusing to give away the bat or let the (soon-to-be-ex) friend borrow the car, I don't *facilitate* them in doing wrong. They might react by doing something wrong, but I'm not helping them do it.

Or consider another case where it seems I should change what would otherwise be permissible behavior in light of others' wrongdoing. Suppose I can easily afford to live in a safe neighborhood. Yet suppose I could save money by moving into a dangerous one in which there is a high chance my children will be attacked on their way home from school. Here it seems plausible that I should not move my family there. In this case, though, the reason is that I have special obligations to my children. These special obligations restrict my freedom in various ways and require me to prioritize their welfare over other concerns. In the same way, I normally have the freedom to play guitar when I feel like it, but it's wrong for me to do so when, say, my son is injured and needs a ride to the hospital. I normally may listen to Slayer when I please, but not, say, when my other son is hungry and needs someone to cook him dinner.

There is arguably also a duty to avoid causing others' peril, at least when that duty can be discharged at a low personal cost. So to take one of Hurd's examples, suppose a railroad knowingly drops a passenger off in a dangerous area when she is not aware of the danger. It does not cause her harm per se. (If she is harmed, the criminals there caused the harm.) Nevertheless, it exposed her to peril when it could have easily avoided that by informing her.[15]

Hurd argues that it's also plausible that we have a duty to modify our behavior in light of others' wrongdoing when the wrongs have already been completed (or the wrongdoers can no longer stop the wrongs from happening). For instance, suppose I see a drunk passed out in the middle of the street. I conclude that he shouldn't be there, so I hit the gas and roll over him. Though I'm right that he shouldn't be there and shouldn't be blocking my right of way, nonetheless he is, and he can no longer do anything about it. I should take his action as a given and avoid hitting him if I can.[16]

Beyond these limited cases (and perhaps a few more limited ones), is it a *general* principle that we lose our rights of self-defense or the defense of others when there is a serious danger that someone might *respond* to our exercising those rights by committing even worse harms? Consider two versions of a yes answer:

- *The Strong Moral Extortion Principle: You should not engage in self-defense or the defense of others whenever there is a serious and credible threat that someone might respond to your defensive actions by committing harm or injustices even slightly worse than the ones you defend against.*
- *The Weak Moral Extortion Principle: You may engage in self-defense or the defense of others when there is a serious and credible threat that someone might respond to your defensive actions by committing harm or injustices slightly or even significantly worse than the ones you defend against. At some point, however, when the threats are severe enough, you have*

> *a duty to back down rather than defend yourself or others.*

Intuitively, the weak moral extortion principle is more plausible than the strong moral extortion principle. It's plausible to think that we have a duty to avoid catastrophe moral horror and that this can override our rights.[17]

Note that the strong version of the moral extortion principle seems to undermine *all* your rights, not just your right to self-defense, far too quickly. Consider that I have the right to draw a picture of the Muslim prophet Muhammad. But I know that if I do so, some extremists might not simply hurt me but might hurt others too. Do I therefore *lose* the right to do that? Similarly, a black man and white woman have the right to cohabitate. Yet suppose they know that if they do so, some racists elsewhere might react by rioting and hurting other people. Do they thus lose their rights to live with each other? If you believe the strong moral extortion principle, there's no obvious reason to limit it only to the rights of self-defense or the defense of others.[18]

SUMMARY

We've examined a number of arguments that attempted to mount a general attack on the moral parity thesis and provide a general defense of the special immunity thesis. Most of the arguments failed because they could not identify a principled distinction between government and nongovernmental wrongdoers: the reasons they gave to avoid defensive actions against government agents were equally good reasons to avoid defensive actions against nongovernmental agents. Further, many of the reasons were not good in their own right. The antivigilante principle, for example, seemed to forbid defensive action even in cases where one could not rely on public defense or restitution, while the fallout objection implausibly held that our rights disappear whenever someone mounts a credible threat in response to us exercising our rights.

At this point we should be skeptical that government agents in general enjoy special immunity against civilians in general. Over the next few chapters, however, I'll explore the more focused question: Does the government (or do certain people in government) enjoy special immunity against its own agents?

CHAPTER 5

Just Say No

THE ETHICS OF FOLLOWING UNJUST ORDERS

In the past few chapters, I've looked at the special immunity thesis in a general way. I've examined and then debunked arguments that attempted to show that government agents (or at least democratic agents) generally enjoy special immunity against everyone else, or at least against civilian citizens subject to that government.

But perhaps special immunity does indeed exist, only in a more limited form. One might say, "In general, sure, government agents are on par with civilians. The conditions under which one can use defensive actions against civilians are also conditions under which one can use defensive actions against government agents. In general, perhaps governments do not have authority over their citizens: they cannot create obligations by fiat. But perhaps a small subset of citizens owes special deference to a small subset of government agents. Perhaps the government has authority over some subset of citizens." The idea here is that instead of holding that all government agents enjoy special immunity against everyone else, some governments enjoy special immunity against some people. The next few chapters will concern this narrower and limited theory of special immunity.

In this chapter, I'll explore what at first glance may seem the plausible instance of this more limited view: perhaps higher-ranking solders (or congress or the chief executive) enjoy special immunity against lower-ranking soldiers.

Perhaps higher-ranking solders enjoy authority over lower-ranking ones. Perhaps high-ranking officials enjoy special immunity against *other* government agents, such as police officers, jailers, spies, intelligence agents, data collectors, and the like. If so, this allows that the government does not enjoy special immunity against us civilians. But it might enjoy special immunity against its own agents, or at least some of them.

If so, this would also bear on what we civilians may do in self-defense or the defense of others against the government. It might mean that we may not, in order to defend others, *become* government agents, and then use our powers or status to sabotage or interfere with government injustice. (In the next chapter, I'll examine this question in more depth.)

In this chapter, I'll look at some arguments that try to generate the conclusion that higher-ranking government agents generally enjoy special immunity against lower-ranking agents, or that agents enjoy special immunity against one another. As far as I can tell, these arguments fail. There is indeed a good case, I'll grant, for maintaining that some government agents have a degree of *authority* over other agents. Yet I'll argue, even if so, there's still little reason to believe that higher-ranking government agents enjoy special immunity against lower-ranking ones.

PROMISES AND AUTHORITY

In commonsense thinking, the act of promising appears to create obligations out of thin air. Many philosophers agree, although some dispute this view of promising.

For instance, I do not have a moral duty to use a red toothbrush. But suppose I promise my wife that I will start using a red toothbrush. It seems that I would suddenly acquire that duty. In virtue of making promises, I can obligate myself to both do certain things and not do certain things.

In virtue of making promises, one can even acquire a duty to *obey* other people. For example, every year Georgetown University commands me (in some loose sense) to teach certain courses. Most people have no duty to heed my dean's commands. If my dean demands *you* serve on the honor council, you may refuse. But in virtue of my contract with Georgetown, I do have some limited obligations to follow some of my dean's orders. I have a genuinely consensual contract with Georgetown. The terms of that contract impose certain duties on both the university and me, and at the same time grant both the university and me certain rights against the other.

Similarly, I could acquire a duty to obey other people by making promises. Suppose I promise a friend, "For the next five minutes, I promise to obey your commands." The friend then asks me to jump up and down once. Due to having made a promise, I should do so.

In chapter 3, we saw that this potential source of government authority does not exist for most citizens. Some philosophers have argued that society is a kind of contract, and we have in one way or another promised the government or each other that we would obey the government. Yet as we saw, the social contract metaphor is inapt.

Some citizens, however, do in fact have special relationships to their governments—relationships that are built on consensual contracts. My neighbor works for the Department of State. Another works as an adviser who meets with the president almost daily. Another works for the Secret Service. Their employment relationship to the government is voluntary, even if many aspects of their general relationship to the government are not. Just as I have acquired some duties to obey certain commands from my superiors at Georgetown, they have acquired some duties to obey commands from their superiors. Just as I have acquired some general duties to do certain things for Georgetown (even in the absence of specific commands), so my neighbor has some general duties to work on behalf of the Department of State.

Similar remarks apply to soldiers in general, or at least to volunteers rather than conscripts. When citizens choose to become soldiers, they become employees of the government. Moreover, they become employees placed in what are often critical and highly important roles. They agree to follow orders and uphold certain standards. In virtue of making such promises, they can acquire obligations that the rest of us lack, including obligations to follow certain orders, behave in certain ways, fight certain battles, and so on.

In the United States, enlisted soldiers take the following oath:

> I, _____, do solemnly swear (or affirm) that I will support and defend the Constitution of the United States against all enemies, foreign and domestic; that I will bear true faith and allegiance to the same; and that I will obey the orders of the President of the United States and the orders of the officers appointed over me, according to regulations and the Uniform Code of Military Justice. So help me God.[1]

Officers make a similar oath:

> I, _____, having been appointed an officer in the Army of the United States, as indicated above in the grade of _____, do solemnly swear (or affirm) that I will support

and defend the Constitution of the United States against all enemies, foreign and domestic; that I will bear true faith and allegiance to the same; that I take this obligation freely, without any mental reservations or purpose of evasion; and that I will well and faithfully discharge the duties of the office upon which I am about to enter; So help me God.[2]

Due to having made such promises, soldiers acquire stringent obligations, including duties to perform unsavory actions that the rest of us would have no duty to perform. They can be required to perform difficult physical labor, endure grueling mental stress, sacrifice themselves to save others, and in some instances kill other people. Similar remarks apply to police officers, Federal Bureau of Investigation agents, and others.

GENERAL AUTHORITY VERSUS SPECIFIC AUTHORITY TO COMMIT INJUSTICE

Recall in chapter 3 one of the challenges to grounding special immunity on authority: it won't be enough to show that government has some kind of general authority. One has to demonstrate that the government has the authority to commit certain injustices—specifically the kinds of injustices one would be justified in using defensive action to stop a private civilian from committing. I've now acknowledged that in virtue of making certain promises or signing certain contracts, governments do indeed have some authority over their *own agents* and employees. But that will not automatically show that these government agents or employees have any duty to allow their employer to commit injustice, or commit injustices on behalf of their employer.

Why not? Well, even if we grant that promises have such magic powers—that promises can introduce or transform our obligations—it does not imply that soldiers, police officers, and the like have obligations to follow unjust orders, or permit *other* government agents to do so. The reason why is that promises cannot *relieve* us of preexisting duties.

Suppose I say, "Hey, everyone reading this book, right now, in virtue of writing this sentence, I hereby promise to murder an innocent Syrian child." I do not, because of making that promise, acquire a duty to murder the child. Nor do I lose my preexisting duty to refrain from murdering the child just because I made the promise.

Similarly, suppose I say, "I, Jason Brennan, being of sound mind, promise to obey my frequent coauthor Peter Jaworski in all things." Suppose Peter and I sign a contract, with me agreeing to follow his orders; in exchange, he pays me $10,000 a month. Now such a contract might in fact obligate me to do *some* things. If Peter demands that I refrain from watching *Game of Thrones*, the contract obligates me to follow. But suppose Peter says, "I demand you murder an innocent Syrian child, and in addition, that you stop feeding your own children." I have no duty to obey Peter here; on the contrary, my preexisting duties to avoid hurting innocent children and feed my own children *trump* my promise.

There is an interesting question, perhaps, about whether I owe Peter some compensation for taking his money after saying I would do whatever he told me to do. But I do not lose my preexisting duties, and others do not lose their rights, just because I made a promise to obey Peter. Syrian children don't lose their rights to life, and my children don't lose their right to be fed, just because I made a weird promise to Peter. Promises don't work like that. They're magical, yet they aren't that magical.

Now one might believe that promises to *governments* are different. But unless we have a good argument to that effect, we don't have any reason to believe it. If I promise to obey the president, and the president then tells me to murder a Syrian child, I don't acquire a duty to kill the child, and the child's rights do not disappear. That's not how rights work. Rights are stringent side constraints held against other people. They do not disappear because you make a complicated promise to someone with a fancy title. The fact that government agents have *promised* to obey the government does not *excuse* them when they obey unjust orders, nor does it relieve them of moral culpability for following those orders. This is a misunderstanding of how promises work.

Let me elaborate. In general, as moral agents, we are subject to a range of negative and positive duties. Negative duties require us to refrain from doing certain things. For instance, we must not kill, torture, hurt, dismember, lie to, steal from, or rape other innocent people. Positive duties require us to do certain things. For example, we should feed our children, reciprocate with those who do us favors, and perform some acts of beneficence. In the middle, we have a range of morally *optional* actions— actions that are neither obligatory nor forbidden. For instance, you may pick whatever color toothbrush you like.

What promises can do (at least according to some of the major theories of promises) is modify the moral status of some of these optional actions. Based on having made a promise, I can convert some actions from optional to forbidden or required. When I promise to pick you up at the airport at 6 p.m., the formerly optional action of picking you up becomes obligatory, and other formerly permissible actions, such as listening to Black Sabbath at that time, become forbidden. But while promises can change the status of optional actions, they cannot change the status of previously forbidden or required actions.

So promising to obey an unjust order, or promising to obey someone who then later orders me to do something unjust, doesn't obligate me to do the unjust thing. But could a promise perhaps obligate me *not* to interfere with unjust actions?

Consider that in commonsense moral thinking, we do not have an unlimited duty to rescue or protect others. Al Gore could spend his millions saving children's lives, but it's permissible for him to spend some of that money on luxury goods, such as a gigantic house or fancy Lexus.[3] It might be heroic for Bruce Wayne (Batman) to stop crime in Gotham City, but it's permissible for him to instead retire to Europe with Selina Kyle (Catwoman).

As we just discussed, promises can change the moral status of optional actions. Acting in self-defense or the defense of others is often, if not always, optional. Thus, can one lose the right to engage in *optional* self-defense or the defense of others in virtue of making a promise to follow orders?

In some cases, that seems plausible. Suppose Batman promises Catwoman that he'll take the night off so they can finally enjoy the Gotham Opera together. It's plausible in this case that he should attend the opera, even if that means he fails to stop some random mugging he otherwise would have had the right to stop.

But consider a more complicated case: What if I get you to promise to do something incompatible with defending yourself or others, and then try to attack others or commit a severe injustice? Here it seems you no longer have to keep your promise to me.

Suppose Batman and Superman are walking down the street. Superman says, "Batman, I'm thinking about retiring. But I know you'd prefer that I keep saving people. So I propose an exchange. I'll spend one more year doing heroic deeds, but only if you promise to do something for me right now. Don't worry, I won't ask you to do anything you are forbidden to do or required not to do." Suppose Batman agrees. Then Superman says, "Ha! Gotcha! What I'm going to do right now is punch that kid over there. Saving that kid from me would have been supererogatory rather than obligatory for you. So, ha ha, you've promised not to stop me!" In this case, it doesn't seem like Batman has acquired a duty not to interfere with Superman. Rather, it seems that Batman's promise did not relieve him of the right to defend others. Or if Superman had said he planned to punch Batman instead, it seems permissible for Batman to defend himself, despite his promise.

Due to making promises, swearing oaths, and signing contracts, government agents and employees do indeed have obligations to their superiors and the government to follow certain orders. A person who commits unjust acts, though, cannot acquire a right that you allow him to commit unjust acts in virtue of getting you to make a promise to obey him, or do something incompatible with defending yourself or others against him. In the case above, when Batman breaks his promise to Superman, it's Superman's fault that Batman breaks the promise, and Superman has forfeited his claim to have the promise obeyed.

FIDUCIARY DUTIES, SPECIAL OBLIGATIONS, AND AUTHORITY

A closely related argument holds that government agents enjoy special immunity against other agents because governments agents are *fiduciaries* of the government, or more broadly, because they have a "special relationship" with the government. Fiduciary relationships appear in cases where one person (or agency, group, department, corporation, etc.) in a position of vulnerability justifiably reposes confidence, reliance, or trust in another person whose aid, advice, or protection is sought. In the law, and plausibly as part of morality as well, when one person is a fiduciary of the other so defined, then the fiduciary acquires an obligation to act for the benefit of the principal (the person/group that justifiably reposes confidence). Some examples of this fiduciary relationship include legal guardians and wards, lawyers and clients, doctors and patients, teachers and students, executors and legatees, priests and confessees, and brokers and clients.

Fiduciary relationships can arise for a number of different reasons. They might develop because of disparities of expertise, such as when patients confide in and trust doctors. They might emerge because of a need for candor, such as when clients confide in lawyers. They might also arise because one person lacks the ability to monitor and control the other, such as when beneficiaries confide in trustees. In some cases, as with stockholders and managers, more than one of these grounds obtains.

Fiduciary relationships require the fiduciary in some cases to prioritize the welfare of her principal over her own welfare and even that of others. For instance, suppose a doctor is prescribing a course of treatment to her patient. Treatment A is much safer and more effective than treatment B. But treatment B costs more; if the doctor prescribes B, it will help her buy a new Mercedes. The doctor has a duty to prescribe A rather than B, or better yet, inform the patient of both A and B, and let her choose.[4]

Or suppose I am consultant advising your firm on a new marketing strategy. Suppose strategy A will help your firm more than B, yet B would come at the expense of shrinking the revenues of another company to which I have no relationship. In this case, I'm required to advise you to do A versus B, as I'm not supposed to take the second company's revenues into consideration.

One might see here a potential opening for holding that some government agents enjoy special immunity against other government agents, or even against contractors, suppliers, lawyers, or others who might work as fiduciaries of the government. If some people bear a fiduciary relationship to the government or its agents, perhaps this requires them to forbear from certain defensive actions.

But this line of argument is no more promising than, well, the promising argument from the last section. The problem is that acquiring a fiduciary relationship cannot relieve us of preexisting moral duties, nor does it invalidate all our rights. At most, fiduciary relationships impose some additional duties on us.

Suppose that Ann is a defense lawyer. She takes on Bob as a client. Bob is being charged with murder. Ann realizes the evidence against Bob is strong and he is likely to be found guilty. Now Ann arguably has a fiduciary duty to help defend Bob, though it's worth noting that some philosophers dispute even that.[5] While Ann can do *some* things to help defend Bob, such as dispute the testimony of a cop she has reason to believe is prejudiced, she cannot just do *anything* to help Bob. For instance, she may not threaten the district attorney's kids in order to get him to drop charges. She may not bribe the judge. Most relevantly, she certainly may not assist the defendant in committing further crimes, and if she has information that he is about to commit a future crime, she must report that, so that he can be stopped.[6]

Consider another example: in business ethics, the stockholder theory of management says that corporate managers are the fiduciaries of the stockholders. Milton Friedman, for instance, argued that because the capital the managers control is *owned* by the stockholders, the managers have a duty to use the capital in ways that promote the stockholders' expressed goals (as defined or constructed by whatever voting procedure the stockholders have). I don't have any stake in stockholder theory, but here I note that one common objection to stockholder theory is based on a crude misunderstanding of the theory.

Some people say, "Stockholder theory cannot be correct, because business managers cannot, say, poison a watering hole or exploit workers just to make a profit for their stockholders." It's true they cannot, but this doesn't show that stockholder theory is wrong. Rather, it illustrates the built-in limits of fiduciary duties. What stockholder theory really says is that managers should use whatever *ethically permissible* means they can to accomplish stockholders' goals, but they do not, in virtue of becoming fiduciaries of the stockholders, acquire permission to violate others' rights or commit wrongs in order to promote their principals' interests.

Further, in virtue of being a fiduciary, a person does not normally lose a right to defend herself or others from her principal. A priest does not have to let the confessee hurt him during confession. A doctor does not have to stand idly by and let her patients murder others. A manager does not have to allow the stockholders to poison the water supply. A guardian can protect other children from her ward. And so on. While our fiduciary obligations require us to prioritize some people's interests over others, they do not require us to forbear from engaging in defensive actions against our principals. They certainly do not require us to *help* our principals commit injustice.

Accordingly, this line of reasoning—that government agents act as the government's fiduciaries—might explain why government agents do indeed have special obligations to the government. But it is not promising as an account of why government agents, such as soldiers or police officers, cannot use defense actions to protect the innocent from other government agents, or stop other government agents from committing severe injustices.

Instead, so far we have good reason to believe that government agents are deeply morally culpable for enforcing unjust laws and orders. A fortiori, when we think about how fiduciary duties work, it's plausible to conclude that a cop who enforces an unjust law is *even worse* than a criminal who performs the same actions. Consider two cases:

1. John decides he doesn't like it when people use pot so he takes it on himself to imprison pot users in his basement.

2. Charlie, a sworn officer of the DC police, throws people in jail who use pot because that's his job and the law tells him to do so.

Assume for the sake of argument that pot criminalization laws are unjust. In my view, Charlie's behavior is *more* contemptible than John's. Charlie, unlike John, is part of an agency that claims a monopoly on the use of violence and claims that right to maintain that monopoly because it will discharge justice. Charlie has sworn to protect people.[7] When John throws people in jail, he's acting like a petty tyrant. When Charlie does it, though, he's not merely acting like a petty tyrant but rather he's in a sense *betraying* us. Charlie isn't just a fiduciary of the government; he's a fiduciary of the *public*.[8]

ESTLUND ON THE MORALITY OF UNJUST ORDERS

In chapter 3, I laid out a general challenge to anyone who tries to justify the special immunity thesis on the basis of governments' putative authority: one has to prove not merely that governments have *some* authority but instead that they specifically have the authority to commit severe injustice—the kinds of injustice we would be allowed to take defensive actions against civilians to prevent. In this chapter (and the next two), I'm considering arguments that try to show *specific* people, rather than people in general, have special duties to the government to follow unjust orders or defer to government agents acting unjustly. This would show that government agents do in fact enjoy special immunity against some people, if not against everyone.

In this section, I'll examine Estlund's attempt to demonstrate that certain government agents have duties, at least in some circumstances, to follow what they *know* to be unjust orders and allow others to execute what they know to be unjust orders. Estlund contends that we have a duty to follow or defer to what we know are unjust orders if the orders were produced by the right people in the right way.

Suppose that the United States conducts a referendum on whether to bomb some target—let's say a military base in Mexico—using conventional weapons, but in this case, it makes a series of "honest mistakes." Suppose Americans mistakenly yet sincerely believe that bombing Mexico is justified according to *the* correct theory of just war, whatever that theory is. Suppose that if their beliefs were correct, it would then be justifiable to bomb Mexico. Suppose they decide to bomb Mexico only after extensive democratic deliberation. But now suppose I happen to know that their beliefs are mistaken and war against Mexico is not justified. Suppose it's *my* job to launch the bombs. Must I bomb the military base, knowing full well that in doing so, I'll hurt innocent people who are not liable to be harmed?

I think it's obvious that I should not do so. Yet Estlund contends otherwise. He claims that when the following conditions are met, a person not only *may* but usually *must* follow orders—even orders to commit what he knows to be unjust acts:

1. The act one is ordered to do is a token of a type of act that could in principle be justified.

2. The decision process used is one that is publicly justifiable to all reasonable people.

3. The order results from a reliable and fair decision process—a process that usually tracks the truth as well as any other process that meets the second condition.

4. Those who issue the order sincerely and in good faith believe that the order is justified.[9]

Estlund takes these conditions to establish both the legitimacy of acting on unjust orders and authority of those orders. He thinks democratic governments are the only types that could meet these four conditions.

Even if Estlund were correct that such conditions could establish the authority of *some* unjust orders and actions, this does not yet justify the special immunity thesis. After all, as Estlund seems to admit, the conditions under which he claims a democracy would have authority are highly ideal, and it's not clear that any actual democracy meets, has met, or will ever meet these conditions.[10] In his book *Democratic Authority*, he never tries to show that any actual democracy has authority; he just tries to outline conditions under which a democracy *could* have authority. So for Estlund to claim that some democratic government agents enjoy special immunity, he'd have to show first that some existing democratic government is sufficiently just and fair to qualify as authoritative, and second that this government has actually issued an order while meeting Estlund's four criteria above. One could accept Estlund's philosophical theory of authority and yet then hold that no government actually has authority because no government meets the required conditions.

This issue aside, should we grant Estlund his theory of the authority of unjust orders? For the sake of argument, I'll assume on Estlund's behalf that he has succeeded in demonstrating that some extant democracies do have a general kind of authority. Even if so, why believe that they could have the specific authority to commit severe injustice? Estlund has two strands of reasoning on behalf of this claim.

First, Estlund relies on casuistic reasoning. He describes a few cases in which a person—Jason the Jailer—is ordered to commit relatively minor injustices. Estlund expects his readers to agree that Jason must obey the orders. He then tries to show that if so, his readers must also agree, on pain on inconsistency, that Jason could be obligated to follow orders to commit relatively severe injustices.

Estlund's least controversial case, in his own eyes, goes as follows. Suppose that a fair and reliable jury in a fair and impartial legal system convicts a defendant, but the jury or judge makes an honest moral mistake. Estlund writes,

> Jason the Jailer realizes the defendant is guilty, but knows that the sentence of 20 years in jail is excessive. Suppose the crime is embezzling $1000. Jason sees that anything more than 5 years is morally indefensible. Jason is legally ordered to keep the prisoner for 20 years, but suppose he could easily let him escape after 5. Is Jason permitted to carry out the full punishment?
>
> It seems clear to me that he is.[11]

Remember that in the case above, Estlund isn't stipulating that Jason merely *judges* or believes that the punishment is too severe. Rather, he wants us to understand that Jason is right and the order is wrong. When Jason judges, "It's unjust to keep the prisoner in jail for twenty years," Estlund stipulates that Jason is correct.

Despite this, Estlund thinks Jason not only *may* carry out the orders (i.e., that he has legitimacy to do so) but also that he *must* (i.e., that the orders are authoritative). The only reasonable grounds for not doing so, Estlund thinks, are if carrying out the unjust order imposes a severe psychological burden on Jason. (That is, according to Estlund, the reason Jason can avoid causing injustice isn't that he's causing injustice but rather that he doesn't have the constitution for it.)

Estlund builds his argument on this kind of case. If you're committed to saying that Jason has a duty to carry out the full punishment here, then, Estlund maintains, you'll have to admit that executioners should kill convicts they know to be innocent and soldiers should follow unjust orders. His main argument is argument by analogy. He tries to show that in certain cases, executioners killing innocent convicts and soldiers following unjust orders are not really different from Jason the Jailer holding the prisoner too long. So on pain of inconsistency, if you agree Jason the Jailer must follow the order to hold the prisoner for too long, you should then agree that others should follow unjust orders. (Again, to be clear, Estlund is not claiming that we must always follow unjust orders. Rather, he's arguing that we must follow unjust orders when they meet the four conditions above.)

For the sake of argument, I grant Estlund that the analogy holds. I'm unmoved, however, by Estlund's example. It seems clear to me that Jason *may* not only allow the prisoner to escape but also, if he's not under duress, *must* allow the prisoner to escape. Estlund also describes a case in which a person is wrongly convicted by a fair and impartial jury trial. The defendant is in fact innocent, but the jury makes an honest, blameless mistake and finds him guilty. Jason the Jailer knows that the defendant is innocent, but despite knowing this, he can't prove it to others. Estlund asks, May Jason let the defendant escape? Estlund thinks that it's obvious Jason may not, but I think it's obvious that he may.

I don't have the moral intuitions that Estlund wants to build on. Thus, when he shows me that the soldiers receiving unjust orders and executioners about to kill innocent people are morally on par with Jason the Jailer, I take that, pace Estlund, as evidence that soldiers must not follow unjust orders (if they can get away it) and executioners must refuse to kill people they know to be innocent, *even if* the orders result from a process meeting the four conditions above.

So Estlund and I have different intuitions here. Is that an impasse? Strictly speaking, that I, a reasonable person, don't share Estlund's intuitions is more a problem for him rather than for me. After all, according to Estlund's own underlying philosophical commitments as a public reason liberal, he needs to justify coercion to all reasonable people. He can't build a theory on controversial intuitions and judgments that reasonable people reject.

By definition, public reason liberals, such as Estlund, Gerald Gaus, Charles Larmore, Rawls, John Tomasi, Jeremy Waldron, and Paul Weithman, accept what philosophers call the public justification principle. (The label for this principle isn't universal; the public justification principle is sometimes called the liberal principle of legitimacy or qualified acceptability requirement.) The public justification principle is a purported moral principle or principle of legitimacy that governs the acceptable use of coercion. Different public reason liberals advocate slightly different versions of the public justification principle:

> 1. *Estlund's Version*: No one has legitimate coercive power over another without a justification that could be accepted by all qualified points of view.[12] (A "qualified" point of view is one that merits a certain kind of respect.)

> 2. *Gaus's Version*: A's coercive interference with B is permissible only if there is a justification for it that B may reasonably be expected to endorse.[13]

> 3. *Rawls's Version*: Political power is legitimate only when it is exercised in accordance with a constitution the essentials of which all citizens as free and equal may reasonably be expected to endorse.[14]

These views are similar but not identical. These philosophers disagree about which disagreements, attitudes, or objections count as "reasonable" or "qualified." Also, Gaus's version of the public justification principle has a wider scope than Rawls's. Gaus's version applies to every act of coercion (whether committed by government or individual people), but Rawls's version applies only to a government's "constitutional essentials." Still, despite these intramural debates, the basic idea is that public justification principle requires that the distribution of political power be acceptable to all reasonable people subject to that power

I invoke this point because it seems that Estlund's commitment puts him at a disadvantage when other reasonable people don't share the basic judgments or intuitions on which he builds his theory. Many reasonable people will dispute that Jason the Jailer has a duty to keep a person in jail for an extra fifteen years. If so, then unless Estlund has an argument that defeats their objection, he should, as a public reason liberal, maintain that Jason's coercive behavior would be unjustified—Jason must not hold that prisoner for an extra fifteen years.

Remember, the fundamental idea underlying the public justification principle is that coercion is presumed unjust, illegitimate, and nonauthoritative unless it is justified in a suitably public way to all reasonable people.[15] On public justification theories, there is a massive asymmetry in what it takes to *justify* coercion versus what it takes to *invalidate* it. Every reasonable person has a special power to block government coercion and invalidate its purported authority.

Also beyond that, it's a part of commonsense moral thinking, by default, that we are presumed not to have a duty to follow unjust orders. This duty has to be justified.

Estlund has a different line of argument—one that might possibly overcome these problems. He contends that disobedience in cases like these involves some kind of wrongful epistemic or moral immodesty. He thinks it can be wrong for you to hold that you have superior judgment to others or certain collective decision processes, or it can be wrong for you to just install yourself as the "boss." For Jason the Jailer to refuse to obey the order would be, in effect, to assert that his judgment is superior to that of the court. Or in effect it would be to assert that he, Jason, is the boss over the court. Estlund adds that even if Jason did have superior judgment, there's no way that Jason could prove to all reasonable people that his judgment was in fact superior.[16]

With this kind of move, Estlund is trying to use the public justification principle *against* the objectors. He might say, sure, Jason the Jailer is right, but people could reasonably dispute that he is right. A soldier might be right that the order is unjust, but people could reasonably dispute whether the soldier has superior judgment. But that's a strange move; after all, Estlund is now requiring public justification for a *failure* to coerce rather than for coercion. The public justification principle, however, applies in the canonical form only to acts of coercion.

I find this argument strange. Jason the Jailer might agree that the legal system is reliable overall and the system tends to be more reliable than he is. Yet he might also hold that in this particular case, it got the wrong answer. And by Estlund's own stipulation, indeed it did, and Jason knows this. What justifies Jason in letting the convict escape isn't that Jason has some specific moral right to always abide by his own judgment—of course, he doesn't—but instead that Jason *got the right answer* while following *correct reasoning procedures*. Talking about who is authoritative misses the point. Jason can let the defendant go not because his judgment that the defendant is innocent is *his* but rather because his judgment is *correct*.

Estlund might say to Jason the Jailer, "You might be right that the defendant is innocent, but who made you boss?" Jason might respond, "I'm not the boss. In this case, *no one* is the boss. The jury justifiably but mistakenly believes that the defendant is guilty. I grant that it has the legitimacy, but not the authority, to jail him. But I know that the defendant is innocent so I must not obey. The reason I can let the convict escape is not because I'm the boss but instead because the jury fails to be my boss." He can let the convict escape not because he, Jason, is authoritative but rather because the government is not.

Estlund's worry about Jason taking himself to the boss might again expose tension in Estlund's thought. Estlund wants to build his theory of democratic authority within the tradition of public reason liberalism. Again, public reason liberalism's fundamental idea is that coercion is presumed unjust, illegitimate, and nonauthoritative unless it is justified in suitably public ways to all reasonable people.[17] Again, on a public reason liberal account, there is a massive asymmetry in what it takes to justify coercion versus what it takes to invalidate it, or in what it takes to justify authority versus what it takes to invalidate it. Every reasonable person has a special power to block coercion and invalidate purported authority. For a reasonable person to reject government coercion needn't mean that he takes himself to be the boss or have authority but rather that he takes the government to fail to be his boss or have authority. When Jason refuses to jail the defendant or helps the defendant escape, he's not coercing anyone, and so his refusal to follow orders doesn't *need* to be publicly justified. The public justification principle does not even *apply* to Jason's actions.

Moreover, it seems that the citizen of a just society would want Jason to let the innocent man go free. Consider a parallel situation. Suppose I believe that the correct moral principles imply that my son Aiden should do X.

But suppose I'm mistaken; in fact, the moral principles imply he should do Y. Now when I tell him to do X, I want him to obey me. But being a decent human being, I also want even more for him to do what's in fact right. As a moral person, I prefer that my son do what's right even though I think it's wrong and ordered him not to, instead of that my son do what's wrong because I think it's right and ordered him to do so.[18] To prefer the latter to the former would be, well, rather vile. For me to prefer the latter to the former would mean I'm more concerned with being the boss than I am with doing what's right.

So similarly, a just democratic society would prefer that its citizens do what's in fact right, even if the democracy mistakenly ordered the citizens to do something wrong, rather than that its citizens do what's in fact wrong because the democracy mistakenly ordered them to do so. Just people say, "Do what's actually right, not what we say is right."

EPISTEMIC DEFERENCE

Soldiers, police officers, and other government agents often have good reasons to defer to their superiors. But it's important, at least philosophically, to be clear on just what the grounds are for deference and what kind of deference this is.

In chapter 3, and in some of the arguments above, we considered whether the government in general might have authority over citizens or in particular whether some higher-level government agents might have authority over lower-level agents. The notion of authority I'm referring to here is what we might call more precisely *moral au-*

thority. Moral authority should be contrasted with *epistemic authority.* Here's the distinction:

A moral authority has a moral power to create duties in another person by fiat. (Here, "by fait" might require that the authority follow some proper procedure.) For example, if my dean commands me to teach the business-government relations course instead of the politics, philosophy, and economics courses I currently teach, I acquire an obligation to do so. Or when people believe there is a duty to obey the law, what they mean is that when lawmakers create a rule, the rest of us have to obey it *because* the lawmakers made the rule. A moral authority is a *boss.*

An epistemic authority has no such powers.[19] Instead, a person is an epistemic authority over you about some issue to the extent that the person is better informed and a more reliable judge of truth than you on that issue. To the degree that the person knows better than you, you have reason to take that person's beliefs and judgments as *evidence.* In some cases, you even have reason to *defer* to that person's judgment. For instance, suppose physicist Stephen Weinberg and I are discussing some issue in physics or cosmology. Suppose he says, "Our current best data indicate the big bang happened 13.7 billion years ago." It would be epistemically immodest for me to disagree with him (unless, say, a bunch of other physicists said he was wrong). When he says that his testimony counts as evidence for me, I have reason to trust his judgment over my own. An epistemic authority is not (in virtue of being an epistemic authority) a boss.

To illustrate this more dramatically, suppose I have a Truth Fairy who rests on my shoulder. Suppose I know that the Truth Fairy is omniscient and never lies. Whenever

I want to know whether a proposition is true or false, I can just ask the Truth Fairy. By hypothesis, I should always believe what the Truth Fairy says. Yet the Truth Fairy doesn't *create* any truths; it just reliably reports them. The Truth Fairy is always right, but she's not my boss.

In some cases, a person might be an epistemic authority concerning *morality*. That is, there might be cases when another person informs you of her moral judgment, it counts as evidence for you that this moral judgment is correct. In some cases, you might even have reason to defer to that person's moral judgment. Here the idea again is not that the person *creates* a moral obligation for you but rather that the person is sufficiently more reliable than you (in this instance, at least) that you should trust her judgment about what is right and wrong over your own.

In some cases, a person might be an epistemic authority concerning morality (over some issue or case) not because she is better at moral reasoning than you but instead because she is more aware of the morally relevant facts. For example, suppose I ask my wife whether some cousin of hers I've never met is a decent person. I should take her answer as evidence not necessarily because I think she's better at moral reasoning than I am but rather because she knows more about her cousin than I do.

In other situations, a person might be an epistemic authority concerning morality over you because she is better at moral reasoning in general or better at moral reasoning in cases like these. Teenagers should take advice from their parents about how to deal with the ethical issues arising in teenage social life because their parents are less biased and more mature. (Teenagers generally disagree, of course.) Or I might conclude that since I haven't thought through or published on just war theory anywhere near as much as, say, Jeff McMahan, I should take that fact that *he* reached certain conclusions as evidence that those conclusions are correct. Or suppose once again I have the Truth Fairy on my shoulder. I ask the Truth Fairy, "Is it permissible for me to buy a BMW rather than save a child's life?" If the Truth Fairy answers yes, then by hypothesis, I now know that I may, even if the Truth Fairy hasn't yet explained to me what goes wrong in, say, Peter Singer's or Peter Unger's arguments to the contrary, or even if I'm too dumb to understand the Truth Fairy's counterarguments.[20]

Now that we have this new concept of epistemic authority in place, we find another set of reasons why police officers, soldiers, and others might have grounds for "obeying" commands from their superiors. At least in some cases, when their superiors issue commands, they should defer to their superiors not because their superiors (or anyone above their superiors) have created an obligation by fiat but instead because they have grounds to believe their superiors are *right* about what ought to be done, as measured by independent moral standards. In some cases, they could even have grounds to defer when they privately judge that what they are being asked to do is wrong.

Consider an unrealistic but illustrative case. Suppose the Truth Fairy and I both join the military. The Truth Fairy is put in charge of my squadron. We are sent to a remote village, inhabited, as far as we can tell, only by old men, women, and children—none of whom are combatants. Now suppose that Lieutenant Truth Fairy says, "You are each morally obligated to shoot these old men, women, and children." Being sensible, we think to ourselves that this seems like the My Lai massacre and what we're doing is evil. Since we know that the Truth Fairy only utters true propositions, however, we also know that our initial judgment is—for some unknown reason—mistaken. Perhaps, unbeknownst to us, these are actually well-disguised enemy soldiers. Perhaps the people are all stricken with the zombie apocalypse virus and we're saving the world. Perhaps there's some other justifying reason. We don't know what the reason is, but by hypothesis, we know there is some such reason.

More realistically, consider a soldier fighting a defensive war against an aggressor. Suppose he lives in a reasonable democratic and liberal state—one that does not have a long history of engaging in atrocities or war crimes. Suppose he gets an order to shoot a missile at a particular target. Above, we explored how in virtue of volunteering to be a soldier, his superiors probably have some degree of moral authority over him, though, as we saw, that wasn't enough to demonstrate that his superiors have special immunity against him. In addition, his superiors probably have epistemic authority as well. If they say that shooting the missile is right, he should also *take that as evidence* that shooting the missile is right because he has grounds to think they are reliable and better informed.

In some situations, certain government agents are more likely to be epistemic authorities than civilians. For instance, suppose once again I am a soldier. My superior officer, whom I know has access to lots of evidence and intelligence that I lack, says, "The right thing to do right now is throw a grenade over that ridge." Simultaneously, I just happen to get a text message from my childhood best friend, who knows I'm a soldier and often sends me random "orders." By coincidence, his text reads, "Hey Jason, if you happen to see a ridge in front of you, you should throw a grenade over it." My superior officer's testimony is evidence that this is what I should indeed do.

My friend's text is not. I have reason to believe that my superior officer has superior knowledge and judgment in this case, but no reason to think that about my friend.

Now does this conceptual apparatus help explain why some superior government agents enjoy special immunity against those beneath them? It seems not. Recall from chapter 2 that the general framework for defensive action goes as follows: one person (the defender) may use defensive action against another (the adversary) when these conditions obtain:

1. The defender is not the aggressor.

2. He reasonably believes he (or someone else) is in imminent danger of severe bodily harm or injustice from his adversary.

3. He reasonably believes that the defensive action is necessary to avoid this danger.

In chapter 2, we explored some of the intramural debates about how broadly or narrowly the details of these conditions should be interpreted. But commonsensically (and in the common law), the reasonable belief criterion was fairly permissive. It did not require that the defender lack any reasonable doubts. It did not require epistemic certainty.

In light of that, one would be hard put to argue that soldiers, police officers, and others are usually forbidden from using defensive actions against their superiors. Yes, they should in some cases regard their superiors as epistemic authorities, and in some cases defer to their superior judgment. But in many or probably most instances, when they are told to do something that seems unjust, it will be reasonable for them to think it is unjust, in which case they may use defensive actions (if the other conditions for defensive action also obtain). To illustrate, the

US soldiers at My Lai might realize that it was perhaps *logically possible* that massacring the villagers was somehow justified in light of some information they lacked but their superiors possessed. Yet it was of course *reasonable* for them to think that massacring the villagers was not justified.

Indeed, the better informed one is about the history of war, statistics on police brutality, psychology of obedience and conformity, and such, the more and more reasonable it becomes to think that when one is being asked or ordered to do something that looks unjust, it is unjust. As a philosopher who can construct thought experiments all day, I can imagine a circumstance in which I would be justified in trusting my superior officer's order to nuke Russia. As a philosopher who is aware of the facts about what people in power tend to be like and tend to do, I also recognize that in any realistic situation where I am ordered to do that, it would not only be reasonable to doubt the order is a good one but unreasonable to accept it.

Similar remarks apply to us civilians. If I had a magic wand that would, say, stop the next hundred drone strikes that the United States launches, I would waive it. Of course I recognize that the military might know something I don't. But in light of the evidence on how the military behaves in general and how drone strikes in particular work, it's at least reasonable for me to distrust its judgment.[21]

CHAPTER 6

Lying with Intent to Sabotage

In previous chapters, I've mostly considered situations in which a civilian or government agent acting in good faith *encounters* an injustice, and then employs defensive actions in response to that injustice. Some of the cases are incidental; for example, Ann is going about her business when she stumbles on someone trying to do something awful. Some involve people at high risk of encountering injustice; for instance, a soldier fighting in a just war receives an unjust order.

In this chapter, though, I'm going to consider cases where people specifically try to *acquire* power by using defensive actions, perhaps with the goal of using this power to perform additional defensive actions. Consider examples such as:

1. Ann takes a job at the Department of Defense with the goal of sabotaging its unjust operations.

2. Oskar seeks out munitions contracts only to have his workers sabotage the product (and thus reduce the military's effectiveness in an unjust war).

3. Edward works as a government security contractor with the goal of gaining access to and distributing documents proving that the state is engaging in serious injustice.

4. Barry runs for president with the goal of undermining voters' unjust preferences and preventing them from getting their way.

5. John attempts to become a juror for a criminal trial with the intention of nullifying an unjust law or hanging the jury.

6. Natalie is nominated to the Supreme Court. Fools control the US Senate. Natalie lies to senators in order to be confirmed.

These cases are more complicated because they involve preemptive defensive actions. In many cases, one has to *lie* to someone about what one intends to do in order to put oneself in the position to do it. For instance, a politician who wants to prevent injustice might need to lie to voters and tell them he plans to commit that very injustice if elected. A potential juror might need to lie and say he will only try the facts of the case, not the law itself. A potential government agent or soldier might need to promise obedience in order to gain the power to disrupt the organization through disobedience.

In some cases, these sorts of lies are morally unproblematic because the potential saboteur lies to the people he intends to sabotage. Suppose it is 1942, for example, and Hitler has already committed many heinous deeds. He offers to hire you as a bodyguard. You lie and swear loyalty to him, with the explicit goal of smothering him in his sleep. Here you lie to someone who deserves to be lied to, or less strongly, someone who has no moral claim not to be lied to. A case like this is unproblematic.

In other cases, however, in order to acquire the office, relationship, or power needed to perform defensive actions, one needs to lie to people who may not be liable to be lied to, or at least, it's not obvious that they are liable to be lied to. For instance, suppose I am considering engaging in jury nullification in response to a person being charged with violating an unjust law. When I am being interviewed as a potential juror, suppose I lie and claim that I would not do such a thing. Here I do not just lie to the prosecutor and judge, who plausibly deserve to be lied to for intending to enforce an unjust law, but also to the defense attorney, who is perhaps not liable to be lied to. Or suppose I am a politician. I perceive that most voters favor racist policies, so I lie and pretend I favor racist policies too, though my actual intention is to win power and then eliminate the racist policies. When I lie, I not only lie to racist voters but also to voters who oppose the racist policies. The racist voters have it coming, but the good voters do not.

I'll start by reviewing the general theory of defensive lying, which I originally discussed in chapter 2. I'll then apply this theory specifically to a defense of politicians lying with the intent to gain power and then sabotage injustice. I start with this case because it is, in a sense, the most difficult one. The reason it is the most difficult is that the kind of power voters have is diffused and indirect, and lying to voters involves not only lying to mean-spirited and malicious voters, or well-meaning but misinformed ones, but also well-informed and well-meaning voters. While I focus here on why politicians may lie to bad voters, the same argument works to explain why other would-be government agents may lie to acquire their jobs so as to prevent injustice.

THE BASIC ARGUMENT IN DEFENSE OF LYING TO BAD VOTERS

Recall, from chapter 2, the basic theory of defensive lying: commonsense morality and most major moral theories hold that lying is only presumptively wrong. The prohibition against lying is not absolute.[1] In the right circumstances, a person is not merely *excused* in lying but also is *justified*.[2]

By default, lying is presumed wrong. Yet a person can become *liable to be deceived* by performing (or intending to perform) certain deeply wrongful, harmful, or unjust actions. A person is liable to be deceived when he is doing (or intending to do) something deeply wrong, unjust, or harmful to others, or to prevent him from causing greater injustice. Defensive lying might also be governed by a doctrine of *necessity*: when a nondeceptive and less harmful alternative is equally effective at stopping the wrongdoer from committing injustice, then perhaps it is wrong to lie. Furthermore, whether defensive deception is merely permissible or obligatory depends in part on whether the potential liar is in danger of retaliation or not. If I can lie with impunity to the murderer at the door, then I should; if the murderer at the door might try to kill me for lying, then lying is permissible (and heroic) but not required. I suspect most people accept this broad outline, though they would dispute some of the exact details of any full theory. (I'll discuss the question of when defensive action is obligatory in further detail in chapter 8.)

With that, now consider a variation on the murderer at the door example. In *The Lord of the Rings*, Gríma Wormtongue, in conjunction with the wizard Saruman, magically manipulates King Théoden into making harmful political choices that endanger the citizens of Gondor. Suppose that something similar were about to happen to our own democratic government. Suppose an evil wizard wants to cast an enchantment on democratic government leaders that will cause them to make harmful political decisions.

The Evil Wizard

An evil wizard has misplaced his magic wand. He knows you know where it is. He asks, "Do you know where my wand is? I need it to cast a magic spell that will magically induce government leaders to implement a number of stupid economic and political policies, thus greatly harming many people."

Here it seems not merely excusable but also justifiable to lie to the evil wizard. Like the murderer at the door, the wizard plans to cause serious harm and injustice, just through rather convoluted means.

Suppose we change the example. Make the wrongdoer a group of wizards as opposed to simply one. Instead of merely lying about a wand's location, you trick them into casting a helpful versus harmful spell. These changes seem to make no moral difference, as in the following illustration:

The Evil Wizard Consortium

A group of evil wizards plans to cast the *hurt people via bad government* spell, just like the evil wizard in the previous case. You cannot stop it from casting a spell. But the wizards forgot the words to the spell. They ask you for the magic words. You have two options. You can give them the words for the *hurt people via bad government* spell. Or you can lie and supply them with the words to the spell *help people via good government.* This spell will magically induce government leaders to produce good policies that in turn produce just and beneficial outcomes. It will also dupe the wizards into thinking they cast the evil spell.

Again, in this case, lying seems at the very least permissible and admirable. Suppose we add in some additional facts: you know you can get away with lying and are not under any threat of retaliation. In that instance, it seems impermissible to tell the truth and perhaps even obligatory to lie.

Now suppose we change the wizards' motives. Suppose the wizards wish to help people, but are misguided about how to do so. Just as misinformed parents might mistakenly believe that refusing to vaccinate their kids helps them, so wizards might mistakenly believe a harmful spell is a helpful one. Just as parents might stubbornly cling to such false beliefs in the face of overwhelming evidence to the contrary, so might wizards.

The Benevolent but Mistaken Wizards I

Some well-meaning but misinformed and irrational wizards want to help people by casting a spell. These wizards mistakenly believe that the spell known as *hurt people via bad government* actually *helps* people. They want to cast that spell in order to help others. If the wizards realized their mistake, they would not cast the spell. For various reasons, though, the wizards in question are too stupid, stubborn, or biased to listen to reason. Any attempt to convince them that the *hurt people* spell actually hurts people fails. They cannot be stopped from casting some spell or other.

Yet they forgot the magic words to the *hurt people* spell and ask you what the words are. You have three options. You can lie to them, giving them the words to the *help people via good government* spell, but tell them that those are actually the words to the *hurt people* spell. Or you can do nothing, in which case someone else will tell them the real words to the *hurt people* spell. Or you can tell them the truth; you can give them the real words to the *hurt people* spell.

The Benevolent but Mistaken Wizards II

Some dumb but well-meaning wizards want to cast the *help people via good government* spell. To cast it, they must first write the words on a scroll and then burn the scroll in the fires of Mount Doom. Being nice but stupid, they mistakenly write down the words for the *hurt people* spell. They ask you to deliver the spell to Mount Doom. You could try to explain to them that these are the wrong words, but experience shows the wizards are too stubborn and unreasonable to realize their mistake. Or you could just promise to deliver their spell, but instead lie and replace their *hurt people* scroll with a *help people* one.

These cases are almost identical. In the first, you lie; in the second, you make a lying promise. In these two situations, the wizards want to help people, but mistakenly desire to do something that will hurt people.[3] In both cases, it once again seems not only permissible but also (unless one is under threat of retaliation) obligatory to deceive the wizards.

In the instances above, the wizards will magically impose bad government on innocent people. In some cases, they want (de dicto) to hurt people; in others, they want (de dicto) to help, but are stubbornly misinformed. Now let's ask, Does it make any moral difference if I replace the wizards with voters and replace magic spells with the democratic process?

The Evil Electorate

A group of malevolent voters wants to use the government to hurt people whom it dislikes. To do this, the voters need to select representatives who will implement various harmful and unjust policies. You can't stop the voters from voting for someone who publicly advocates such harmful policies. Yet you can trick them into thinking that *you* advocate these policies, even though you don't. Once elected, you can then refuse to implement their favored policies and instead implement good ones.

For instance, suppose they support an unjust war or Jim Crow laws. You can lie and tell them you do too. Once in power, you can just refuse to either start the war or impose Jim Crow. The good news is that the voters are probably too dumb to notice that you tricked them, so you can probably get away with it in the long term.

The Benevolent but Dumb Electorate

A group of dumb but nice voters wants to use government to help others and promote justice. To make this happen, the voters need to select a number of good representatives— that is, representatives who will implement policies that will in fact produce beneficial and just outcomes. Nevertheless, the voters are ignorant, uninformed, misinformed, and irrational in how they process social scientific information. Thus they have mistaken beliefs about what it takes to help people and produce just outcomes. They will only vote for politicians who pledge to support what are in fact bad policies—policies that would undermine rather than help the voters' own deepest goals. You are in a position to trick them, though. You could lie to them and tell them that if elected, you will implement their favored harmful policies. Once elected, you could instead impose good policies—policies that will in fact help people and produce beneficial outcomes. The good news is that the voters are probably too stupid to notice that you tricked them, so you can probably get away with it over the long haul.

At first glance at least, these two cases seem analogous to the wizard cases above. In both the wizards and electorate cases, a group of people intends (whether out of malevolence or misinformation) to cause great harm and injustice. The groups should therefore be considered liable to being deceived. If deception is necessary or the best way to stop them, then it seems that lying is at the very least permissible and perhaps (if one can lie with impunity) even obligatory. Perhaps there is a good enough disanalogy between the cases, however, or perhaps there is something special about voters that makes them not liable to being lied to.

ARE VOTERS ACTUALLY LIKE THE BENEVOLENT BUT MISTAKEN WIZARDS?

Above I compared the electorate to the benevolent but mistaken wizards. Here I explain briefly why I think that's an apt analogy, at least at first glance.

I begin with some good news about motivation. Political scientists overwhelmingly find voters tend to vote sociotropically rather than selfishly.[4] That is, they tend to vote for what they *perceive* to be in the national interest rather than in their self-interest. Voters desire de dicto to help, not hurt, others.

That said, there is plenty of bad news about ignorance and misinformation. As political scientist Philip Converse summarizes it, "The two simplest truths I know about the distribution of political information ... are that the mean is low and the variance is high."[5] (The mode and median are also low.) Legal theorist Ilya Somin, author of *Democracy and Political Ignorance*, says, "The sheer depth of most individual voters' ignorance is shocking to many observers not familiar with the research." In his extensive review of the empirical literature on voter knowledge, Somin concludes that at least 35 percent of voters are "know-nothings."[6] Political scientist John Ferejohn agrees: "Nothing strikes the student of public opinion and democracy more forcefully than the paucity of information most people possess about politics."[7]

For example, during election years, most citizens cannot identify any congressional candidates in their district.[8] Citizens usually don't know which party controls Congress.[9] During the 2000 US presidential election, slightly more than half of Americans knew Gore was more liberal than Bush, but did not seem to understand what the word liberal meant. Significantly less than half knew that Gore was more supportive of abortion rights, more supportive of welfare state programs, favored a higher degree of aid to blacks, or was more supportive of environmental regulation than Bush.[10] Only 37 percent knew that federal spending on the poor had increased or crime had decreased in the 1990s.[11] On these questions, Americans did worse than a coin flip.

Similar results hold for other election years.[12] The American National Election Studies surveys eligible voters on basic political information, such as who the candidates are or what these candidates stand for. On this test of *basic* political knowledge, the top 25 percent are somewhat well informed, the next 50 percent do little better or worse than chance, and the bottom 25 percent are systematically misinformed (they make systematic mistakes and do worse than chance).[13]

Note that these statistics are just on measures of *basic political knowledge*—easily verifiable facts such as what the unemployment rate is or who the incumbents are. Voters fare even worse on tests of social scientific knowledge such as economics, sociology, or political science— the knowledge needed to form sound policy judgments. Most voters would not only fail economics 101 but would make systematic errors too.[14]

Political knowledge makes a major difference in how voters vote and what policies they support. Martin Gilens, Scott Althaus, and Bryan Caplan, for instance, each using different data sets, find that low- and high-information voters have systematically different policy preferences, and these different preferences are not explained by demographic differences.[15] Misinformed or low-information voters tend to support what social scientists (both on the Left and Right) consider destructive social, military, and economic policies. For example, Gilen notes that high-information Democrats have systematically different policy preferences from low-information ones. High-income Democrats tend to have high degrees of political knowledge, while poor Democrats tend to be ignorant or misinformed. Poor Democrats approved more strongly of invading Iraq in 2003. They more strongly favored the Patriot Act, invasions of civil liberties, torture, protectionism, and restricting abortion rights and access to birth control. They are less tolerant of homosexuals and more opposed to gay rights.[16]

Voters are not merely ignorant or misinformed but also epistemically irrational. The field of political psychology finds that most voters suffer deeply from a wide range of cognitive biases. As political psychologists Leonie Huddy, David Sears, and Jack Levy observe, "Political decision-making is often beset with biases that privilege habitual thought and consistency over careful consideration of new information."[17] These biases include motivated reasoning, intergroup bias, confirmation bias, and availability bias, among others.[18] In general, voters tend to form political beliefs on the basis of little to no evidence, and then stick to those political beliefs no matter what new evidence they encounter. They regard those with whom they disagree as moral monsters. Few process political information in a minimally rational way.

To be clear, how voters vote is not the only thing that determines what policies governments will impose. For a wide variety of reasons, government bureaucracies, agencies, and politicians have significant freedom in imposing or implementing policies against voters' wishes.[19] What government does is not simply a function of voters' will. This book assumes that how voters vote makes some significant difference, but if that were false—if voters' votes didn't matter much at all—then there would be no reason to lie to them, as by hypothesis, doing so would be unnecessary to protect the innocent from wrongful harm.

LYING TO BAD *AND* GOOD VOTERS

There is at least one crucial disanalogy between the benevolent but dumb electorate in the case above and real-life electorates. In the case above, everyone in the electorate is benevolent and dumb. In real-life electorates, the overwhelming majority of voters are benevolent and dumb, but a small minority is benevolent and smart. Thus, if a politician were to lie defensively to voters, she will not only lie to dumb voters who are liable to be lied to but also to smart voters who are not. Is that reason to think lying is wrong?

I think not. To see why, consider another type of murderer at the door case:

Murderers and Heroes at the Door

You are hiding Jews in your attic who are escaping persecution. Six people knock at your door at the same time. Five of them are SS agents hoping to find and execute any hidden Jews. One, you realize, is from the resistance and is hoping to help Jews escape. When the SS agents ask you if you're hiding Jews, if you lie, you'll end up not only lying to them but also lying to the agent from the resistance who is trying to help.

In a case like this, if you lie, you not merely lie to people who are liable to be lied to but also to an innocent person who is not liable. Indeed, by lying, you might undermine another person's heroic efforts.

Nevertheless, in lying, you most likely don't *harm* the person from the resistance, and it still seems like a justifiable or at least excusable response under duress. The agent from the resistance may dislike being lied to. Yet given that you and he share the same goals—to protect Jews from being killed—he would most likely have no complaint that you lied to him in front of SS agents. At most he might complain if you were not acting strategically— that is, if this were a case where lying was likely to backfire rather than work.

Further, you also have the *duress* excuse: an innocent person will be captured and killed unless you lie to an innocent person—a person not liable to be lied to. Your lie does not harm the innocent. In this case, it seems, you are justified in lying to the SS agents and *excused* in lying to the double agents.

Consider a variation on this case:

Murderers and Innocent Bystanders at the Door

You are hiding Jews in your attic who are escaping persecution. An SS agent knocks at your door. You open it. He asks, while standing outside, if you are hiding any Jews in your house. Behind, walking on the street, there just so happen to be two innocent bystanders; indeed, you happen to know that these two people are the nicest and most innocent people who have ever lived. They turn to listen to your response. You lie to the SS agent, and in so doing, lie to the innocent bystanders as well.

By hypothesis, the bystanders are not liable to be lied to. They don't have it coming. When you lie to the SS agent, you also end up lying to them. (If you object that they are not really being lied *to* but simply being lied *in front of*, you can change the case by imagining they also ask you, at the same time, whether you are hiding Jews.) Still, by lying to them, you are unlikely to harm them, you likely save a life, and you are acting under duress. Lying to them seems at least excused, if not justified.

If you accept these judgments, then you can apply similar judgments to cases of lying to the electorate. Suppose (correctly) that the majority of voters are misinformed, and hence support dangerous, harmful, and unjust policies—policies that they would not support if they were better informed—while a minority are well informed and support good policies. If a politician lies in order to get elected and then imposes good policies, she will have lied not only to bad voters who have it coming but to the good voters as well. At least she will not have harmed the good voters, however, and she can compare her situation to the murderers and philanthropists at the door case. She can say to the good voters, "I'm sorry I had to deceive you, but if I'd told you the truth, the bad voters would have gotten their way, and we all would have suffered."

For some reason, when we switch out evil wizards for evil voters or misguided wizards for misguided voters, most people's judgments change. In their view, there is something special about voters, making it wrong to stop them from hurting innocent people. While defensive lying is permissible against evil or benevolent but dumb wizards, it is impermissible against evil or benevolent but dumb voters, although the wizards and voters seem to be doing the exact same thing.[20]

People must thus hold that the wizard and electorate cases are not closely analogous, or that there is something about an electorate that gives it special immunity against defensive lying. As I will argue below, though, there are no good grounds for believing either.

"THEY'RE ONLY HURTING THEMSELVES" AND PURE PROCEDURALISM

Let's turn to considering potential explanations for why voters enjoy a special immunity against defensive lying. One purported disanalogy between the wizard and voter cases goes as follows:

> The evil wizards hurt *other* people. The voters only hurt themselves. People have a right to hurt themselves, and we should not stop them from doing so.

That people have a right to hurt themselves seems plausible. If I eat five bags of Cadbury Mini Eggs daily, I might develop diabetes. But it's plausible to hold that I have a right to eat myself to death, and no should interfere with or stop me from doing so, however imprudent it may be.

This objection fails because it's not true that bad voters are just hurting themselves. An electorate is not a unified, unanimous body whose decisions only affect itself. In every democracy, some people impose their decisions on others. Bad voters hurt the smart and well-informed minority of voters, people who abstained from voting, future generations, children, immigrants, and foreigners who are unable to vote yet who are still subject to or harmed by that democracy's decisions. For instance, Americans' propensity for military intervention hurts Iraqi children, not just Americans. Political decision-making is not choosing for oneself; it is more like choosing for everyone.

Moreover, even if (contrary to fact) voters were "just hurting themselves," there might be *some* cases where paternalistic lying is permissible. Suppose Bob is about to eat a candy bar containing a fatal dose of cyanide. You tell him it contains cyanide, but he thinks you're joking. Yet suppose if you lie and say it contains peanuts (which he's allergic to), he will believe you. In this case, it seems at the very least *excusable* and perhaps justifiable to lie to Bob. One can imagine analogous cases involving politicians and voters.

Closely related to this objection is another one that holds it is a mistake to say that it is unjust for the majority voters (out of malice, ignorance, or irrationality) to impose harmful government on others. Instead, some democratic theorists are attracted to a view called *pure proceduralism*. Pure proceduralism maintains that there are no independent moral standards for evaluating the outcome of the decision-making institutions. So, for example, Habermas holds that so long as we make and continue to make decisions through a particular highly idealized deliberative process, any decision we make is just.[21]

The motivation behind pure proceduralism is typically that since people disagree about what justice requires, democracy is the fair way to resolve their disputes. But as Estlund has pointed out, this does not give us any particularly good reason to prefer democracy; we could fairly decide political outcomes by rolling dice or flipping a coin.[22] Beyond that, pure proceduralism has some deeply implausible implications. According to a pure proceduralist, so long as democracies arrive at a decision through the right decision-making method, then whatever they decide is for that reason just. Yet this implies that if a democracy were to follow the right procedures, and then as a result, decide to impose Jim Crow laws, start a nuclear war against Haiti, legalize infant rape, and assign citizens to marriages by government fiat, these policies would therefore be just. On reflection, few people would be willing to bite such bullets. It's instead much more plausible that in a wide range of cases, there is an independent truth of the matter about what democracies ought or ought not do.

PUBLIC REASON AND SINCERITY

Many political philosophers now endorse the public justification principle, which claims that coercive political power is illegitimate unless it could be justified to the individuals subject to that power "by their own lights" or on the basis of reasons they could, in some way, "recognize as valid."[23] Just what this principle amounts to is hotly debated.

In the first instance, the public justification principle is meant to be a partial theory of political legitimacy: coercive institutions are legitimate only if there are certain undefeated, publicly available reasons in favor of them. Some advocates of public justification, however—although by no means all of them—go further, and claim that the principle also constrains politicians' and/or citizens' speech by limiting the kinds of arguments they may make in public about politics.[24]

To my knowledge, Micah Schwartzman provides the strongest, most thorough defense of the claim that the public justification principle requires politicians to be sincere. If Schwartzman is right, and if the public justification principle is right too, then this could be a problem for my thesis. I happen to think the public justification principle and theories built atop it are false and implausible, but since these theories remain popular, I pause here to examine whether my thesis is incompatible with these theories.

Schwartzman wants to ground the duty of sincerity on the epistemic benefits of public deliberation. His first premise is that citizens cannot deliberate well unless the reasons for various proposed political actions are public. His second premise is that democratic deliberation will tend to "improve the quality of political decisions." According to Schwartzman, this premise is "the linchpin of his argument." From there, Schwartzman adds a few more premises and goes on to conclude that politicians must be sincere.[25]

Rather than reiterate and evaluate Schwartzman's entire assertion at length, I will take him at his word that this second premise—that public deliberation among citizens tends to improve the quality of political decisions—is indeed the linchpin of his argument. If so, then his argument seems to fall off the axle.

It is almost tautological to assert that ideal deliberators—perfectly rational, unbiased people who decide only on the basis of reasons and process evidence in a scientific way—would make better decisions after deliberating. But whether real-life deliberation among real-life citizens improves the quality of political decisions is an empirical question, which depends on political psychology.

In fact, political psychologists and political scientists have produced a massive body of empirical work on how democratic deliberation actually proceeds, and what it actually does to people. The results are largely discouraging for deliberative democrats. For instance, in a comprehensive survey of all the extant (as of 2003) empirical research on democratic deliberation, political scientist Tali Mendelberg concludes that the "empirical evidence for the benefits that deliberative theorists expect" is "thin or non-existent."[26] More recent research continues to vindicate this conclusion; only a minority of the experiments find positive results.[27] As political scientist Diane Mutz remarks after reviewing this research, "It is one thing to claim that political conversation has the *potential* to produce beneficial outcomes if it meets a whole variety of unrealized criteria, and yet another to argue that political conversations, as they actually occur, produce meaningful benefits for citizens."[28]

It is thus unclear how Schwartzman's argument applies to real-world democracy. Schwartzman might be right that it's wrong to lie to (and hence sabotage) good deliberators, but those aren't the people I'm talking about here. I'm talking about actual voters and deliberators out there in the world who meet the standards of good deliberation roughly as well as I meet the standards for membership in the Avengers.

Even if these worries were swept aside, at most the public justification principle would forbid *some* lies, but not all of them. Remember, the fundamental idea underlying the public justification principle is that coercion is presumed unjust, illegitimate, and nonauthoritative unless it is justified in some suitably public way to all reasonable people.[29] On public justification theories, recall that there is a massive asymmetry in what it takes to *justify* coercion versus what it takes to *invalidate* it. Every reasonable person has a special power to block coercion and invalidate purported authority. At most the public justification principle implies that when a politician lies, he thereby fails to publicly justify any coercive actions he defended on the basis of those lies, and so these coercive actions are illegitimate. But the public justification principle leaves open that the politician could lie in order to *stop* coercive policies from being implemented. The whole point of the public justification principle is to make it difficult to *impose coercion*, not to *stop coercion*. Coercion needs to be publicly justified; noncoercion does not. The sincerity objection, if right, only forbids the politician from imposing coercion on the basis of lies, but it doesn't forbid him from lying to stop others from imposing coercion.

To illustrate, suppose voters want to start an unjust war, impose Jim Crow, and implement deeply harmful economic protectionism. Suppose I make a lying promise to voters that I will do each of these things when elected president. When, after being elected, I refuse to start the war, oppress blacks, or stop people from buying Korean cars, I do not coerce anyone but rather fail to coerce people. Thus, my nonactions do not fall under the scope of the public justification principle. Even if the public justification principle (as Schwartzman believes) somehow forbids insincerity, it only applies to cases where I lie in order to coerce, not cases where I lie in order to stop coercion. It would not apply to these cases.

THE SLIPPERY SLOPE OBJECTION: CAN WE ALSO HARM VOTERS IN SELF-DEFENSE?

One final worry about my argument is that it may lead to even more radical conclusions. The argument I advance is based on the doctrine of defensive lying, which is itself isomorphic to the doctrine of defensive killing. One might make the following objection:

> If voters' actions constitute a serious threat of causing unjust harm, then it should not merely be permissible to lie to them. According to the argument, bad voters are analogous to a block of wizards casting a harmful spell. If so, then if necessary, it should be permissible to harm the wizards in order to stop them. But that seems false. If so, then we should be suspicious of this line of reasoning. Perhaps voters do enjoy a special immunity against being harmed or killed, and if so, then perhaps they also enjoy a special immunity against being lied to.

In short, the worry here is that if it's implausible to think voters could be appropriate targets of defensive violence, then by extension, it's implausible to think voters could be appropriate targets of defensive deception.

On the one hand, perhaps this slippery slope is worth the slide. I can at least imagine circumstances in which it would not seem absurd to think voters are rightful targets of defensive violence. Imagine, for example, that my small democratic city-state is about to vote on whether to launch a nuclear weapon against a defenseless neighboring city-state. Suppose the attack is wrong, and suppose that I know every other voter except for me is dead set on launching the attack. Suppose the missile will fire as soon as the vote finishes. In that case, I might not judge it impermissible to, say, take defensive action to prevent voters from reaching polling places to stop the vote. But realistic examples of voting are almost never like this.

But if in principle, in certain cases, voters could be rightful targets of defensive violence, in real-life modern democracies, it's almost impossible to find these kinds of case. Consider that according to the commonsense theory of defensive violence, one of the conditions for defensive violence against someone liable to defensive violence is that it must be *necessary* to stop him from committing the severe injustice. The necessity condition at the very least means that there is not an equally good and effective nonviolent means of stopping that person. One reason why violence would rarely be permissible against voters is that this necessity condition will rarely obtain.

First, politicians could *lie* to voters instead, as they often do. Violence is a last-resort defense; it's at most permissible if lying and other sorts of defensive sabotage don't work. The claim that politicians may lie to dangerous voters does not lead down a slippery slope to the assertion that vigilantes may kill them; instead, it may be that the possibility of lying to voters is one of the things protecting voters from being rightful targets of violence.

Second, the necessity proviso of the doctrine of defensive killing also calls for minimizing the amount of violence. To stop wrongdoers from committing a severe injustice or harm, one shouldn't kill five hundred thousand people who are liable to be killed when just a few would be equally effective. So when violence is justified against state agents, it will most likely have to be targeted at a small number of people. For instance, suppose voters vote to maintain slavery as a legal practice and support politicians who in turn support the Fugitive Slave Act. Now suppose that I see an officer about to capture an escaped slave. It seems plausible to me that I use violence to prevent the officer to make sure that the slave stays free.[30] But it's hard to see how killing southern voters would help or be more effective than taking action against the people who enforce the law.

One might think that these responses invalidate the argument for lying to voters. After all, if defensive violence should be more closely targeted, then so should lying, right? There's something to this worry, and it represents an important caveat. If there are other, more effective ways to stop bad and unjust policies from being implemented than by lying to voters, then we should indeed use these other ways.

It's also plausible, however, that the conditions under which it's permissible to lie are significantly less stringent than those under which it's permissible to use defensive violence. One reason for this is that defensive lying will frequently (perhaps usually) not cause harm to anyone, while killing and other forms of violence do. As I discussed earlier in this chapter, when you lie to both the SS agents and the person from the resistance, you don't *harm* the agent from the resistance. The stakes in justifying violence are much higher than they are for justifying lying.

Suppose we are having a referendum on whether to nuke the island nation of Tuvalu for fun. Suppose polls reveal the majority of voters support nuking Tuvalu. If, in order to stop the referendum from taking place, I bomb the polling places, I will most likely kill, injure, and maim a large number of innocent people. Lying to voters, in contrast, will just cause them to have false beliefs and is not likely to cause any significant harm.

The slippery slope objection gets something right. My general claim here is that voters do not enjoy a special immunity against being lied to. I would similarly endorse the claim that voters do not enjoy special immunity against being killed. Instead, I'm happy to accept that what it takes to justify lying to or killing nonpolitical agents is the same as what it takes to justify lying to or killing political agents, though of course I've only argued against special immunity to being lied to in this chapter. Still, the point is that it's much harder to justify killing or hurting other people (regardless of whether they are private civilians, political agents, or civilians performing political activities) than it is to justify lying to them. The conditions for justifiable violence are far more stringent. Accordingly, the slope between "you can lie to bad voters" and "you can kill bad voters" is not so slippery.

SABOTAGE, BUT DO YOUR JOB

In previous chapters, I discussed how you cannot acquire permission, let alone an obligation, to do something wrong just because you take a job, promise to follow orders, or agree to fulfill a role. If you promise to do what your boss orders, and your boss orders you to put people in jail for something that should not be a crime, the problem is that you made too broad of a promise—a promise that you should not have made. Promises, taking on roles, taking a job, or becoming a fiduciary can constrain or change the status of what were, before the promise, optional actions, but they cannot relieve us of prior obligations.

In this chapter, I've used variations on the murderer at the door thought experiment to show that politicians can lie to bad voters. This is perhaps the hardest case to justify. But similar arguments apply to, say, a person joining the Drug Enforcement Administration with the intent of sabotaging the unjust war on drugs or the National Security Agency with the intent of whistle-blowing on its unjust invasions of our personal privacy.

Yet many such government agents are asked to do a mix of both just and unjust things. They are asked to do both mundane work that someone in government needs to do as well as unjust things that people ought not do.

In general, if you take such a job, you acquire an obligation to perform the *permissible* functions of the job. To take a cartoonish, unrealistic illustration, suppose the Nazi government advertises a position. This position has two responsibilities: in the morning, execute Jews, and in the afternoon, make sure welfare checks go to mothers with dependent children. For the sake of argument, suppose the second action is a legitimate function of government, and suppose that if the person taking the job doesn't perform it, the mothers and their children won't eat. As I asserted above, you could lie to get the job with the intention of sabotaging it. When you show up in the morning, you must not kill Jews. After your lunch break, though, when you switch to the afternoon portion of the job, you should perform that function competently. The reason is that you promised to do so, and your promise is binding in this case. Now if performing the second, legitimate duty somehow interfered with you stopping Jews from being executed, that would excuse you in failing to send the checks. But otherwise, you should do the permissible portion of your job faithfully and competently, even while you refuse to do the unjust portion. (If you think the Nazi regime is so bad that no promises to it can bind, then switch this out for a more mundane case, such as a US police officer being asked to arrest drug users as well as murderers. He should do the latter but not the former.)

Similar remarks apply to realistic police officers, judges, federal agents, and so on. If you become a police officer in the United States, you'll be asked to do both just things (such as escort social workers when they rescue children from abusive homes) and unjust things (such as arrest people for possessing marijuana). You should do the legitimate part of your job competently and in good faith, because you agreed to do so and accepted the role. This part of your promise binds. But you must not perform the unjust actions.

CHAPTER 7

Vigilante Justices

WHAT JUDGES SHOULD DO IN RESPONSE
TO UNJUST LAW

In this chapter, I consider one last—and at first glance, most perplexing—set of cases: I ask what *judges* and *justices* may do in response to unjust laws.

In most countries, judges are asked not simply to apply and enforce the law but to interpret what the law means as well. Consider the following examples:

1. Suppose a criminal is justly convicted of a crime that he in fact committed. But suppose the minimum legal penalty for the crime set by the legislature is unjustly severe.

2. Suppose a person is found guilty of a crime, but the proscribed activity should not be a crime. For instance, the United Kingdom charged mathematician and computer scientist Alan Turing with "gross indecency" for his consensual homosexual relationship.

3. Suppose you were a US Supreme Court justice in 1856, and you were asked to decide the *Dred Scott v. Sanford* case. Among the things you have to determine are whether black people whose ancestors were imported into the United States can be US citizens, whether such people have legal standing to sue in federal court, and if the federal government has the authority to prohibit and

regulate slavery in federal territories. Suppose that (according to the correct theory of constitutional interpretation, whatever that is), the Constitution clearly indicates that such blacks cannot be citizens, cannot sue, and the federal government cannot prohibit slavery in the territories.

My view is that in cases like these, judges may refuse to enforce the law or may even *lie* about its content.

The basic argument for this claim is simple. People have rights. If a constitution or law fails to recognize those rights, or permits rights violations, the constitution or laws have to give way, not people's rights. Our rights impose constraints on what others may do to us. They constrain what laws they may pass and enforce. They constrain what counts as legitimate or authoritative constitutions, if there even are such things. When there is a conflict between our rights and the law, judges may ignore the law and instead do what justice requires.

INTERPRETING THE CONSTITUTION VERSUS DOING THE RIGHT THING

Many modern governments follow the United States' lead in both adopting a written constitution, and codifying citizens' rights within that constitution. The purpose of doing so is in part to show that rights are not like other laws. For the government to interfere with such rights takes a special degree of scrutiny and justification.

The writers of the US Constitution certainly did not believe that rights *come* from the document. They didn't think that in adopting the Bill of Rights, they were *creating* rights by legal fiat; rather, they thought they were codifying preexisting rights and helping to ensure that the legal machinery would recognize such rights. Indeed, during the federalist versus antifederalist debate, many federalists opposed adopting a bill of rights because they believed that such a bill would cause future judges or generations to believe mistakenly that our only rights were those outlined, listed, and codified in the bill. Their view was, "We better not make a list of rights, because we might accidentally leave something important off. Future legal theorists might mistakenly conclude the only rights we have are the ones we listed."

But this brings us to the main question of the chapter. Certain people, such as judges and justices, district attorneys, and police officers, have jobs in which they are required to *interpret* or *apply* the law. This leads to an interesting question: What should they do when asked to interpret or apply unjust laws or constitutional clauses? Notice there can be a conflict between identifying what the law in fact is and doing what's just. If so, perhaps there are times when what judges ought to do is deliberately misinterpret the law—that is, lie or misrepresent what the law says.

One of the major debates in legal theory concerns how supreme court or other judges ought to interpret written constitutions or laws. Here the "ought" isn't a moral ought. Rather, it refers to what they ought to do if they want to determine what the law really is.

There are of course many competing theories of constitutional and legal interpretation, including:

- *Original Intent Theory: The law should be interpreted as meaning or being consistent with what the people who drafted or ratified the law intended it to mean.*
- *Original Public Meaning Theory: The law should be interpreted as meaning or being consistent with what*

reasonable people at the time of ratification would have understood the text of the law to mean.
- ***Living Constitution / Loose Constructionist Theory:*** *Holds that the constitutional law should be understood to evolve and change over time in light of society's changing understandings or moral views.*

And so on. There are perhaps a dozen major theories of constitutional interpretation. Similarly, there are a large number of views in legal theory of what makes a law a law—that is, what distinguishes a law from a mere command, or what distinguishes a *real* law from, say, a law that's "on the books" but not really enforced.

I am agnostic about which theory of constitutional or legal interpretation gets the law right. Thus, I take no stance on *which* theory of constitutional interpretation or law is correct except insofar as I reject any review in conflict with the following claims. In my view, the law is a purely sociological phenomenon. Even if moral nihilism (the view that there are no moral facts or truths) turns out to be correct, there are still such things as laws. Further, it is a coincidence, for lack of a better word, if there is any overlap between what the law allows or forbids and what justice allows and forbids. That is, an unjust law (such as a law permitting slavery, forbidding homosexual sex, criminalizing caffeine consumption, or imposing protectionist tariffs) can certainly be law. Perhaps it is essential to the concept of law that for something to be a law, people must generally regard it as authoritative. I take no stance on that. But that's compatible with holding that in fact no laws have any actual authority. I take it that the claim "the Fugitive Slave Act was indeed the law, but no one should obey or enforce it" is a coherent sentence. These commitments might perhaps rule out a few theories of constitutional interpretation, such as certain extreme versions of natural law theory, but they are compatible with most of the major ones.[1]

The question of what's the *correct* way to identify the content of the law, however, is distinct from the question of what you ought to do, morally speaking, if someone asks you what the law is. Consider a cartoonish parallel case. The philosopher Immanuel Kant was anything but a lucid writer. There's a large literature trying to interpret what Kant meant by this or that. There's also a large literature espousing metatheories of how to interpret Kant. Suppose (contrary to fact) that I happen to be the world's best Kant scholar; unlike all those other poor schmucks wasting their careers, I actually have gotten Kant right and understand how to read him. Now suppose that in a bizarre turn of events, some rival Kant scholar asks me what I think Kant meant at 6:430 of the *Metaphysics of Morals*. I know he's jealous of my Kantian interpretation skills. So I know that if tell him the truth about *Metaphysics of Morals* 6:430, he'll punch me in the face. According to the doctrine of defensive lying, I may lie to him. My right of self-defense permits me to lie about the interpretation of Kant.

Now consider a similar case, this time involving the defense of others:

The Interpreter

The famous philosopher of language Ann is out for a walk. Some people come up to her and hand her a piece of paper. They say, "Hey, Ann, we regard that piece of paper as authoritative; we believe that we are morally required to do whatever it says. But we have a hard time interpreting it. We know you're an expert on this kind of thing and are asking you to interpret it for us. We're going to do whatever you tell us the document says." Ann realizes that they are absolutely sincere. Ann reads the piece of paper, and it says, in plain English, "Go ahead and enslave people." The truth of the matter, according to the correct theory of language interpretation, is that the piece of paper indeed says, "Go ahead and enslave people." Ann lies and tells them, "It says you must not enslave people and that you should not treat others as you would not wish to be treated."

Ann lies to her audience, but she does the right thing. The paper in fact says that the people should feel free to enslave others. She recognizes that it says that. She is not "interpreting" the paper as saying that it forbids slavery. Rather, she *lies* and says it forbids slavery, though it doesn't. The reason she does so is because she recognizes that lying to them would stop them from committing a great evil. They are like the murderers at the door.

Note that I'm not here making the stronger claim that Ann has a duty to lie. Perhaps it's permissible for her to instead reply, "Well, the piece of paper says you may enslave people. But you shouldn't do that, even if the paper says so. There's no reason to do what the paper says. Only vile scum would regard a piece of paper as morally authoritative." Here I only claim that Ann is *permitted* to lie. Whether she is *obligated* to lie is another matter, open for debate. (I'll discuss this further in the next chapter.)

I expect most readers would agree. If so, then consider some examples from constitutional law. *Dred Scott v. Sanford* led to horrific injustice. (The 1857 US Supreme Court decision held that black persons, even free blacks, whose ancestors had been imported and sold as slaves could not be US citizens and could not have standing in federal court.) Yet it's quite plausible to think it was "correctly" decided in the sense that the judges interpreted the case the way prior case law and the Constitution required.[2] For the sake of argument, let's grant that the decision was "constitutionally correct," meaning that the decision against Scott is what the correct theory of legal interpretation, whatever that is, would require in this case. Nevertheless, it was permissible for the judges to either refuse to enforce the Constitution on the grounds that it is evil, or lie and say the Constitution in fact favored Scott.

Now consider a different case. Suppose the US Supreme Court has to hear a case on whether gay marriage should be permitted. For the sake of argument, suppose it is unjust to fail to recognize gay marriage. But suppose also that according to the correct theory of constitutional interpretation, the Constitution does not require the government to recognize gay marriage. Here the judges may feel free to lie and say that the Constitution requires the government to recognize gay marriage.

In both cases, the reasoning is simple:

1. We may lie to the murderer at the door (see the last chapter).

2. The justices' situation is sufficiently analogous to the murderer at the door scenario.

3. Therefore, the justices may lie.

Justice imposes constraints on law, not the other way around.

Some may object, though, that judges or justices have unique circumstances. Below, I'll consider some objections to my thesis.

EXTREME LEGALISM AND PURE CONVENTIONALISM ABOUT RIGHTS

I presume that most people believe that when a (written or unwritten) constitution or the law fails to recognize our rights, we still have those rights. Constitutions and various legal structures may codify our rights as well as help protect them but they do not in general *create* them of thin air or make them vanish by forgetting to mention them. You have a right to free speech because that's what justice requires, not because your country's constitution says so.

Still, even if you agree that our rights exist independently of the law, you might think that convention or law can determine some of the fine details of what counts as our rights. For instance, you might believe that as a matter of justice, people have a right to engage in consensual sex with other adults. At the same time, however, you might hold that what counts as the age of consent is, within a reasonable range, a matter of convention. You might think that as a matter of justice, people should be allowed to own property, but they can forfeit property by abandoning and not using it for long enough. Yet you might think that the number of years it takes for property to revert back to the commons is, within a reasonable range, just a matter of convention. On this view, law-independent moral norms fix the broad contours of our rights and justice, but the law or other conventions can decide the fine details.

Some nevertheless might hold the more extreme perspective that rights are mere artifacts of constitutions or the law. On this view, if the law fails to declare that we have such rights, then we simply do not have them. If the

United State repealed the First Amendment, then Americans' freedom of religion would instantly vanish. The government could then, without injustice, mandate everyone convert to Catholicism or Pastafarianism.

There are three possible views of where rights come from and to what degree they are conventional:

1. *The Pure Natural Rights View*: Our rights are, in every aspect and detail, independent of social conventions, laws, and the state.

2. *The Moderate View*: Certain broad aspects of our rights are natural—that is, independent of conventions and laws; other aspects and details of our rights, however, must be settled by conventions or laws.

3. *The Extreme Legalist / Pure Conventionalist View*: Our rights are in every aspect and detail *dependent* on government-created laws.[3]

Note that the labels don't matter here. If you find phrase "natural rights" irksome, use a different word or label. The point is that the pure and moderate view holds that our rights are not entirely determined by legal fiat or social convention.

On its face, the moderate view is the most plausible. I won't argue here against the pure natural rights view; if that view is correct, it helps rather than hurts my argument. But I will criticize the extreme legalist view below.

Someone who accepts the moderate view could allow that the law can create *legal* rights where there were not any before, provided that doing so does not violate people's preexisting moral rights. So a moderate natural rights theorist could grant that my children have a legal right to state-funded education *because* the law says so. The natural rights theorist is only committed to the view that some of our rights are preconventional, not that all of them must be.

But if the extreme legalist / pure conventionalist perspective were correct, then what rights we have would be entirely dependent on government-created laws. One might think that the extreme legalist view would pose a problem for the moral parity thesis, and that such an outlook would tend to favor the special immunity thesis. After all, if our rights are entirely a legal fiat, then the government gets to decide what our rights are, and it seems it could just decide we don't have a right of self-defense against it.

More precisely, whether the extreme legalist view is compatible with the moral parity thesis or not is contingent. It depends on what laws a given regime has actually passed. Suppose the extreme legalist considers some regime legitimate and authoritative. Now suppose that regime's constitution says that people have no right of self-defense. According to the extreme legalist, as a result, no one would have a right of self-defense. Yet the moral parity thesis would still hold, trivially: we would have no right to fight back against either government or civilian assailants, and so they would be on par. Or suppose the regime says specifically that Jews lack a right to life, but everyone else has that right. In that case, the extreme legalist view would hold that no one has the right to defend Jews from either civilian or government assailants, but would still allow that everyone else can defend themselves along with any non-Jews from both civilian and government assailants. So this law would be compatible with the moral parity thesis. Imagine instead that the government issued a law saying, "Everyone has the right of self-defense and the defense of others against civilians, but no such right against any government agents acting ex officio." In that case, the extreme legalist would say that the special immunity thesis is true and the moral parity thesis is false. So to summarize, whether the extreme legalist view is incompatible with the moral parity thesis depends on what the law is.

The extreme legalist perspective has some unpalatable consequences. Consider the following example:

The Hermit

You are exploring the world when you come across an unidentified island. You check your maps and databases, and determine that the island is not under any government's jurisdiction, nor is it under any sort of international law. You discover that the island has a sole hermit living there alone. You decide to burn down his garden, pillage his hut, torture him, and then kill him, just for fun.[4]

The extreme legalist view holds that in this scenario, you do not violate the hermit's rights. By hypothesis, he lives outside any legal jurisdiction; no legal jurisdiction or laws declare that he has any rights. The extreme legalist must conclude that the hermit simply does not have any rights. But this seems like an absurd consequence. Absent an extremely compelling argument for extreme legalism / pure conventionalism, we should reject it. What the extreme legalist would need to do is give us a powerful argument that makes us skeptical of the idea that people have any rights at all other than as a matter of convention or legal fiat. I'll examine some attempts to generate that conclusion in the next few sections.

The extreme legalist might try to respond as follows: "No, in the case of the hermit, he in fact is the legal authority in his hut. He is like a king in a one-person kingdom. So he indeed has rights." But that won't work. Suppose before you murder the hermit, you ask him whether he believes in rights or has ever decreed that he has rights. He says, "Oh no, I'm a rights skeptic. I think the idea of natural rights is nonsense on stilts. In fact, I don't believe in right or wrong. I'm a moral nihilist, though I have no intention of harming anyone." That wouldn't license you to burn down his garden, pillage his hut, torture or kill him, and so on.

The most plausible view is that people have certain rights, and these rights are not merely legal fiat. Sometimes constitutions and laws *recognize* or codify people's preexisting rights, and at other times legal regimes fail to do so. People nonetheless have rights.[5]

There are interesting philosophical debates about precisely *which* rights we have and why we have such rights. Moreover, there are interesting debates about whether these rights are absolute or merely pro tanto—that is, whether rights can be overridden by other considerations. (For instance, if a cop or Batman must commandeer your car to stop a terrorist, may he do so?) Yet these debates aim to discover the truth about rights, not to *create* the truth by fiat, as if we could decide arbitrarily whether people have a right to life, or simply choose to make rights stronger or weaker on whim.

SOME CONCESSIONS AND CLARIFICATIONS

As I discussed above, the moderate view of natural rights holds that the *core* of our rights is, in a sense, preconventional, but it allows that the fine details of our rights might be decided by convention. There are decisive, preconventional reasons to think that people have a right to life, to avoid enslavement, and so on. But exactly how such rights will work might properly be determined through convention or even legal fiat. So, for example, I take it that the right to property is not merely a matter of arbitrary legal convention; the fine details, such as how many years it takes for a person to acquire property through adverse possession, is largely a matter of convention.[6]

Thus, the moderate can say something like this: "If a Supreme Court justice has to hear a case on how long adverse possession should take, she can feel free to reference previous case law, the Constitution, and convention. There are preinstitutional limits on what the judge can say. For instance, she may not conclude that adverse possession takes only ten seconds, as that would be incompatible with our having any real property rights. Within a certain range, though, she should decide based on what the laws says. There is no higher truth to appeal to."

Further, the moderate can accept that in some cases, citizens might forfeit some of their rights. The moderate might hold that we should in general act as though citizens retain their rights unless they go through some sort of reliable procedure for assessing whether the citizens have forfeited their rights. Suppose, for instance, that O. J. Simpson in fact murdered Nicole Brown. Now the doctrines of self-defense and the defense of others say that Nicole could have killed O. J. to protect herself. Had you been there during the attack, you also could have killed O. J. to save Nicole. Yet the attack is over and Nicole is dead. The jury found O. J. not guilty. A moderate might say something like, "Even though O. J. in fact committed the crime and thus deserves to go to jail, since the court found him not guilty, none of us should treat him as if he'd forfeited his right to freedom. For example, we shouldn't lock him in our basement." (Locking him in your basement is private punishment, not self-defense or the defense of others.) In chapter 3, I outlined reasons to be skeptical of whether government has authority in general. But strictly speaking, this concession makes no difference to my argument here. After all, if you tried to kidnap and imprison O. J. in your basement as he walked out of the court, you wouldn't be acting in self-defense or the defense of others. (He did not represent any immediate threat.) You would instead be engaging in private punishment.

Let's consider another complication. One might reason as follows:

> Judges have to be careful when "lying" about the law or refusing to enforce it. After all, they might face retaliation for doing so. They might be impeached and removed, or otherwise stripped of their office. Or the public might refuse to listen to them. It may be that if a judge lies on a minor case, she will lose the opportunity to stop even greater injustices. For instance, if an abolitionist low-ranked judge wants to have a chance of becoming a Supreme Court justice (a position in which she could criminalize/abolish slavery), she might have to "go along" with perpetuating minor injustices.

In the abstract, we can state the judge's dilemma here as follows: the pursuit of local optima can prevent the judge from achieving global optima. Maybe she has to save her defensive actions for the right time.

I suspect saying so is starting to get annoying, but note once again that you can take any number of stances on this issue and still endorse the morality parity thesis. After all, private civilians can face similar problems. They are statistically unlikely to face this dilemma, but they nevertheless could. Suppose Ann sees a bully stealing a kid's lunch. Yet suppose she knows that a different bully is likely to commit an even worse act in the future—she's

heard rumors that this other bully plans to beat up another kid later. She also knows that if she intervenes now,
she'll be sent to the principal's office and will not have
the opportunity to intervene later. So she decides that she
will not intervene now but instead wait to intervene in
the future case. We might debate this issue, yet it's at least
plausible that Ann can wait and has a good excuse not to
intervene now.

Regardless, the larger point is that judges and laypeople can face the same problem. There's no difference in
principle. Rather, the difference is statistical: judges are
much more likely to encounter this sort of dilemma. But
presumably the same moral principles govern both cases.

That said, things are more complicated if the justice
does not simply *fail* to stop injustice but instead helps
cause it. (Moreover, in some cases it's unclear whether a
judge is failing to stop an injustice or causing it.) Suppose
Ann is a lower-level judge. She wants to get promoted to
a position where she can push for the abolition of slavery. In order to do that, she needs to avoid being too much
of an activist now—she has to go along with the system
or she'll never be confirmed to the Supreme Court. Today
she hears a property theft case. The defendant is found
guilty; she agrees he was indeed guilty. But suppose her
state has unjustly harsh penalties, requiring her to give
him a minimum of twenty-five years in jail, while the
truth is she should give him only a few months. If Ann
decides to enforce the sentence, she not only fails to use
defensive actions to protect the convict from injustice.
Rather, she herself commits an injustice now so as to be
in position to stop a greater injustice in the future.

Is that permissible? Whatever you think the answer
is probably has no bearing on whether you accept the
moral parity or special immunity thesis. Here the issue

isn't whether it's harder to justify self-defense against government agents but rather whether rights are "side constraints" or not. In *Anarchy, State, and Utopia*, Nozick argued that a theory of justice could give rights a central place but still fail to think about rights the right way.[7] Imagine a "utilitarianism of rights." This theory holds that we ought to do whatever *minimizes* rights violations. Nozick complains that this utilitarianism of rights still fails to take rights seriously. This theory would still sanction frequent and serious rights violations, provided that doing so leads to fewer net rights violations. For instance, the US government spies on us, but claims to do so to stop *others* from violating our rights even more. So Nozick would conclude that the US government cares about rights, but not the right way.

Nozick argues instead that rights are *side constraints*: they tell us what we *can't* do. Sure, all things being equal, we should choose institutions and actions that tend to minimize rights violations, but we should do so without first violating others' rights. The *nonviolation of rights* trumps the *protection of rights*. To give an example, suppose (I think contrary to fact) that allowing the FBI to engage in warrantless wiretapping tends to minimize the total rights violations. A side constraint view of rights would maintain that this is wrong; the FBI cannot *violate rights* in order to minimize the violations of these rights.

For what it's worth, Nozick suggests that rights are perhaps not absolute.[8] Rights are side constraints, so we cannot infringe a right simply because doing so will lead to net fewer rights violations. But perhaps, Nozick suggests (though he does not take a stand), we can infringe rights to prevent *disasters* or "catastrophic moral horror."[9] On this view, you shouldn't steal $100 from me to buy the gun you'll use to stop someone else from stealing

$101. But perhaps you could be excused for stealing my airplane to fly it, *Independence Day*–style, into the invading aliens' mothership.

ARGUMENTS FROM DISAGREEMENT

People—including the world's best judges and political philosophers—disagree about what rights we have. In this section, I'll consider a variety of objections holding that in one way or another, the fact of disagreement shows judges should not lie about the law.

To start with, some philosophers and political theorists seem to think my way of thinking about rights is a nonstarter. They might advance the following argument:[10]

The Argument from Disagreement

You, Brennan, seem to want to ignore, evade, or deny the political. Politics is the realm of moral dispute. We need democratic politics precisely to decide which rights we have, because the very rights we have are in dispute. We cannot refer to some procedure-independent moral truth.

At first glance, this perspective seems committed to a strange kind of moral relativism and for a strange reason. As we tell our philosophy 101 students, the mere fact that people disagree about some issue does not automatically imply that there is no truth of the matter or that every side is equally valid. People dispute all sorts of things—the theory of evolution, that the earth is over ten thousand years old, that free trade is usually beneficial to all sides, or that $0.9999... = 1$—about which we have decisive evidence for one side.

Instead of holding that moral disagreement entails there is no procedure-independent truth about what rights we have and thus that we should settle the dispute through procedural means, why not instead conclude we should *avoid* political means? Consider this parody:

> Politics is the realm of moral dispute. The very rights we have are in dispute. For that reason, we should be wary of the democratic political process. After all, by hypothesis, lots of people dispute that you have the rights you in fact have. There's a real danger that if we subject this question to the democratic political process, it will be used to deprive you of your rights.

Someone who believes in rights might think this is a *better* response to the problem of disagreement. People have rights, so we should remove questions about rights from the political bargaining table in order to protect those rights.

Let's take a step back. Consider the two claims I've labeled A and B below. Many people think that A in some way tends to lead to or provide reasons to believe B, though A doesn't quite *imply* B.

A. What rights we have are subject to persistent dispute.

B. We should let the political process determine what rights we have.

There is a big gap between A and B. Let's consider two possible routes from which you could get from premise A to conclusion B. One way to fill in the gap is with a theory called pure proceduralism. Another, more plausible way is with a theory called instrumentalism.

As stated, the argument from disagreement seems committed to a kind of radical pure proceduralism about rights. Pure proceduralism holds that there are no independent moral standards for evaluating the outcome of the decision-making institutions. So, for example, Habermas contends that so long as we make and continue to make decisions through a particular highly idealized deliberative process, any decision we make is just. Or as the political theorist Iñigo González-Ricoy says, "In a democratic society no process-independent moral criteria can be referred to in order to settle what counts as a harmful, unjust or morally unjustified exercise of the right to vote, for voting is a device that is only called for precisely when citizens disagree on what counts as harmful, unjust and morally unjustified."[11] Notice how strong of a claim González-Ricoy seems to make: people disagree about what counts as harmful or unjust. Therefore, he concludes, we may not refer to any independent standards of justice by which to judge what democracies do.

Pure proceduralists believe that there are some objective, procedure-independent moral norms that constrain political decisions, but these norms constrain only *how* we make political decisions, not *what* we decide. Pure proceduralists hold that there are procedure-independent moral truths about *which* procedures we must use to make decisions, and that's it.

But this commits them to some strange and unpalatable conclusions. Suppose we follow the proceduralists' favored decision procedure, whatever it might be, and then conclude that we should nuke Tuvalu for fun. The proceduralist would have to say that the decision is therefore just, legitimate, permissible, or whatnot. Yet that seems absurd.

Pure proceduralism is a bizarre view, and I'm not sure anyone really asserts it, despite writing in favor of it.[12] Some people who defend pure proceduralism—such as Jeremy Waldron, Jürgen Habermas, Iñigo González-Ricoy, Ian Shapiro, and Chantal Mouffe—seem not to accept it in their other papers. For example, in most of Waldron's work (except on political participation and disagreement), he defends substantive claims about what is just or unjust, and admits he might be wrong. But to my knowledge, he never argues for his conclusions the way a pure proceduralist should. He never writes, "In this paper, I defend the claim that X is just. My argument is that it turns out we decided last year that X is just. Therefore X." Rather, he makes procedure-independent arguments and writes as if he were tracking an independent moral truth. A genuine pure proceduralist, though, could never defend a substantive theory of justice other than by stating, "This is what we decided." A genuine pure proceduralist would defend substantive claims about justice not with philosophical arguments but rather with a historical report or survey data.

A more plausible route from A to B is *instrumentalist*. In the abstract, *instrumentalism* holds that there are procedure-independent truths of the matter about what rights we have or about what justice requires. An instrumentalist advocates using whatever decision procedure in politics (or outside it) that best tends to track this truth. So while a pure proceduralist might say something like, "We have these rights because our democracy says so," an instrumentalist would reverse this and say, "We should implement democracy because democracies tend to respect our rights better than other forms of government."

An instrumentalist might modify the argument from disagreement as follows:

The Stability Version of the Argument from Disagreement
Look, we're more or less stuck having to live with one another, despite our disagreements about rights and justice. We should use some nonviolent, stable way to resolve

our differences as much as possible so as to reach a position that we can live with free of violence or constant disobedience. We don't want people fighting on the streets. Democratic decision methods give people a psychological sense of buy in. In a democracy, people generally feel that their voice has been heard and respected, even if they don't get their exact way. As a result, democracy tends to be the most stable and effective way to resolve disagreement. Social change is close to impossible in a society where most people oppose the change.[13]

Here the instrumentalist does not deny we have rights, nor does the instrumentalist purport that democracy settles or decides the truth about justice. Instead, the instrumentalist is making an empirical claim about how stable democracy is and why. Fair enough.

Still, an instrumentalist making this sort of argument can grant that *because rights matter*, we would should use peaceful, democratic decision procedures only as much and insofar as they in fact tend to respect as well as protect our independently defined rights. The instrumentalist could then accept my argument in this book. Sure, we should have a liberal democratic regime, with judicial review and other checks, because such regimes tend to have peaceful transfers of power and respect rights better than other systems. At the same time, individual citizens may engage in self-defense or the defense of others, because such resistance *enhances* the system by stopping government agents from violating as many rights or committing as many injustices as they otherwise would.

Still, the objection gets something right. Social cohesion is itself a value. We understand in our daily lives that we should live with some slights—a derisive comment from an in-law or a guy answering the phone at the movies—

rather than police every wrongdoing. So it may go with certain trivial infractions (whether by civilians or government agents) of our rights.

Another instrumentalist version of the argument from disagreement might go as follows:

The Democratic Deference Version of the Argument from Disagreement

People disagree about what rights we have. Yet when a large number of people opine, through the democratic process, that we have a particular set of rights, this is evidence that those are in fact our rights. The democratic process doesn't invent rights out of thin air. Rather, it is a reliable way of *discovering* which rights we have. Democratic decisions, collectively, are pretty smart. And we as individuals are not. So since the democratic process is fairly reliable, you should defer to it, and assume that when you disagree, you're wrong, not the democratic body.[14]

In chapter 5, I discussed cases where soldiers receive what appear to be unjust orders, but have reason to believe their superiors know more than they do, and this extra knowledge explains why the order is not in fact unjust. This current argument is a variation on that same theme: it maintains that judges might believe that the law is unjust, but they should recognize that because it was produced by a reliable, truth-tracking process, the law is more likely to be correct about what justice requires than their own judgment.

This objection is easily brushed aside, though, because it relies on an unrealistic depiction of how democracies work. As I noted in chapter 6, most voters are systematically ignorant, irrational, and misinformed about politics.

The reason they behave so badly is that their individual votes count for little. They are neither rewarded for being smart voters nor punished for being dumb ones. They can afford to indulge ignorance and misinformation, and use their votes expressively. Furthermore, empirical work on voting behavior finds that few voters have a real ideology or set of political beliefs; most vote one way or another not because they agree with a party's platform or ideology but rather because that's what people like them do.[15] Partisan loyalties are not much based on political *belief*; if anything, political belief is based on partisan loyalty. Postelectoral politics is based more on trading favors and rents than anything tracking important moral truths.[16]

A better variation of the previous argument goes as follows:

The Common Law Deference Version of the Argument from Disagreement

The common law is a largely spontaneous body of law that evolved over a thousand years. Judges had to decide cases with a mind to what is fair and just as well as to find solutions to problems that would solve problems and enable disputing parties to stop fighting and get on with their lives. When judges made good and useful decisions, other judges would copy them. The use of juries and competition between alternative courts also ensured widespread and smart input from the masses. Accordingly, the common law represents the wisdom of the masses. The common law's decision-making process encourages *smart* decisions, unlike the democratic process, which encourages bad ones. A judge should be extremely cautious about overturning a common law principle; it's more likely he's wrong than the common law is.[17]

This, I think, is the best instrumentalist argument for judges to defer to the law. To be clear, it doesn't hold that the law has authority because it's law; rather, it claims that the judge should regard the process that gives rise to the common law as reliably tracking independent moral truths and dependably created conventions that deserve respect because they solve real-life problems.

But note that this assertion does *not* say that judges must defer to the law when they *know* it's wrong. Instead, it says that they should be extremely cautious in overturning common law precedent that they believe is wrong because they should recognize the common law is more likely to be correct than they are.

This seems correct to me, and brings us back to an important caveat that I made in chapter 1: we must be cautious when using defensive actions. In certain cases, we may be biased in thinking that defensive action is called for even when it's not. (In other cases, though, we may be biased in thinking it's not called for when it is.) While statute and democratically decided laws are not determined by particularly truth-tracking or reliable processes, common law does not suffer from the same incentive problems that plague laws made in legislatures and democratic bodies.

All that being said, it's already *part* of the common law tradition that judges may overturn past decisions and revise the past law. Judges are supposed to exercise caution, and they internalize and abide by a number of principles that help inform them when to defer to past decisions versus when to rely on their own judgment that these decisions were wrongly decided or at least no longer binding.[18]

In the end, this is compatible with my main thesis. When law and justice conflict, judges should do what's just. Yet it's also crucial for them to recognize that their *judgment* that the law is unjust may, in certain cases, be unreliable, and so they should exercise extra caution before acting on that judgment.

SUMMARY

Much of what I said in the last chapter applies equally well to judges. Just as politicians may lie to bad voters to gain office, so judges may lie to bad politicians or bad voters to gain office. The argument is more or less the same.

This chapter considered a number of new challenges to the moral parity thesis, focusing in particular on arguments that might show judges are in some way special. The worry was that perhaps the state or its agents enjoy special immunity against its judges and justices, even if the state does not have special immunity against most other people. But once again, the arguments did not quite work. Some were nonstarters. Others were more like clarifications of my own thesis; specifically, the common law deference argument explains why judges should be cautious in legislating from the bench, but is compatible with my thesis.

CHAPTER 8

Must You Resist?

SOME CLOSING THOUGHTS

In the first seven chapters, I defended the moral parity thesis and debunked the special immunity thesis. These first seven chapters established that people are permitted to defend themselves and others from government injustice, and that the principles governing self-defense or the defense of others against government injustice are no stricter than those governing self-defense against civilian wrongdoers. Government and its agents are not magic. They are not surrounded by some moral force field that requires us to suffer injustice at their hands anymore than we must suffer injustice at the hands of our fellow citizens.

Some philosophers, however, think we not only have moral permission to resist but also a moral obligation to do so. We need to distinguish between two ways of understanding this putative obligation:

> 1. *Perfect Duty*: You are obligated, at least prima facie, to act in self-defense or the defense of others whenever you have the opportunity to do so.

> 2. *Imperfect Duty*: You have a general obligation to act to reduce the amount of injustice in the world, but you have significant leeway to determine how and when to make your stand. You don't have to spend your life fighting injustice and defending others. At a certain point, you've "done your share" in fighting injustice.

Perfect duties refer to duties we must strictly observe at all times. The manner in which we observe them is not up to us. For instance, my obligation to respect others' right to life is a perfect duty. It's not I get to choose when and where to observe the duty. It's not as though at some point—say, around age fifty—I'll be able to proclaim, "Well, I've done my share of refraining from assault, so now it's clobbering time." Rather, I must always and everywhere respect people's rights to life. Similarly, the obligations not to steal or lie are also perfect duties.

Note that perfect duties need not be *absolute* ones. To say that a duty is absolute is to say that it can never be overridden by a contrary consideration. Yet as a matter of definition at least, it's possible that *other*, more important duties could override perfect ones when such duties come into conflict. Thus, we can hold that the duties not to kill others or lie to them are perfect, even though these can be overridden by other considerations, and even though in some cases wrongdoers can at least temporarily forfeit their right not to be killed or lied to. Indeed, as I discussed in chapter 2, people can become liable to be killed, harmed, or lied to in certain circumstances. When you kill someone in self-defense, you don't violate that person's right to life because that person does not at that moment hold such a right against you.

In contrast, imperfect duties are those that we must fulfill, but that grant us significant personal prerogative in determining how we fulfill them. For instance, the duty to act benevolently does not require you to continuously aid everyone who needs it but rather in general gives you significant space to determine how and when you will aid others. If, as many people believe, there is a duty to exercise civic virtue, this does not call for any particular action; you could discharge that duty in any number of ways, such as by voting well, writing letters to the editor, volunteering, or arguably, even fixing motorcycles or making doughnuts.[1] If, as Kant thought, there is a duty of self-improvement, this does not require us to spend all our time working to improve our virtues and skills, even when we have nothing else to do. Instead, it just means that from time to time, we should work to improve ourselves.

In this chapter, I want to argue that in general, you do not have a perfect duty to resist injustice. In chapter 2, I described a number of cases of defensive action (cases A–M and A'–M'). While in each case Ann's defensive actions were permissible, she was probably not *obligated* to engage in these defensive actions (although cases H and H' might be the exceptions, as I'll explain below). Ann's actions are heroic, but she would not have been blameworthy in these cases for failing to defend herself or others.

I'll nevertheless leave open whether there is something like an imperfect duty to resist oppression and act to reduce the amount of wrongdoing in the world. Toward the end of the chapter, I'll look at recent papers by Carol Hay and Daniel Silvermint, both of whom contend that there is a duty to resist oppression. While I'm skeptical that either philosopher succeeds, as we'll see, they both argue that there is only an imperfect versus perfect duty to resist.

My view is that civilians in general have significant personal prerogative to get on with their lives. You do not become a conscript into the Army of Justice as a result of being victimized or being around injustice. Perhaps in special circumstances, however, either when you have special obligations to particular people or when stopping a particular injustice is of sufficiently low cost to you, then you have an perfect obligation to resist a specific injustice.

The story for government agents may be different. Government agents have voluntarily placed themselves into positions of special responsibility. In virtue of making certain promises to protect and serve the populace, they owe us more than the typical civilian does. Further, government agents are often in good position to sabotage or undermine government injustice without suffering negative consequences. When one cop sees his partner engage in excessive violence, for instance, he could easily jump and stop him. If you, a civilian, attempted to do so, the cops might kill you. But a cop isn't going to shoot his buddy when his buddy tells him to calm down.

SUPEREROGATION?

Rosa Parks refused to give up her bus seat for a white passenger. She helped to start a civil rights revolution, though her cause is not yet fully won. She's a hero.

That we think she's a hero is at least some evidence that we also regard her actions as supererogatory. To say an action is supererogatory is to say that it is morally good and deserving of praise, but not *required*. It goes *above and beyond* the call of duty. It goes beyond what we think we can thanklessly expect of you.

We do not say, "Well, that was the least she could do." Maybe Parks would say that about herself. Heroes often downplay their heroism. They often feel compelled to take a stand. They sometimes claim they were just doing what anyone would have done. If only that were so!

Parks was a hero, but did she *have* to be a hero? We don't seem to blame the thousands before her who, in the face of oppression, sat in the back. It thus seems strange to say that Parks was merely doing her duty while all the other compliant passengers were failing in their duty. If we really thought that, then we would probably not praise or remember Parks but instead would condemn the others who followed orders and suffered oppression. (In the same way, no one celebrates that I have never murdered my wife; that's just my duty. But we remember and condemn spouse murderers.)

One might object that on the contrary, there are special cases where we consider people who do their duty heroic. Imagine a person is under significant duress—the kind of duress that would normally excuse them from doing their duty—but does the duty anyway. For example, Hugh Thompson refused to kill My Lai villagers and ordered his troops to shoot any US soldiers troops who interfered with his rescue. There is a sense in which he was merely doing his duty. We think Jean Valjean is heroic for keeping his promise to rescue Cosette when obsessive Inspector Javert is in pursuit. But what makes doing one's duty in these cases heroic is that the actors were under significant duress. They were in mortal danger and had *excuses* not to do their duty.

Perhaps one might hold the same view of Parks. Maybe she did have a duty to say no, and so did most of the other oppressed black passengers—but they were all under serious duress. They would have been excused (at least somewhat) in failing to stand up for themselves.

So here are two competing ways of describing Parks's actions:

1. Her conscientious refusal to comply with the law was supererogatory.

2. Her conscientious refusal to comply with the law was obligatory, but since she was under duress, it would have been excusable to comply, and thus doing her duty was still heroic.

I'm worried that taking a stance on either description amounts to splitting hairs. Either way, the upshot is that we would not consider *failure* to resist in cases like this as blameworthy, and we consider resistance heroic. So for the rest of this chapter, I will remain indifferent about these two competing ways of describing resistance:

1. In general, civilian resistance is supererogatory.

2. In general, civilian resistance is a duty, but since most agents who resist are under significant duress or face serious danger, it would be excusable for them not to resist, and so their resistance is heroic.

Again, the situation for government agents is different. Parks lost her job at a department store because she didn't comply with racist rules. This gives her an excuse: she might be unjustly punished for doing the right thing. But now suppose you are a government agent ordered to do something unjust. If you fail to comply, you might lose your job too. Your situation is different from Parks's. You took a job that you should have known carried significant moral risk; you volunteered to be in a position where you might have to say no on pain of losing your job.

ONE MOTIVATING IDEA: THE INNOCENT SHOULD NOT HAVE TO BEAR THE COSTS OF INJUSTICE

In the popular movie *Office Space*, the character Michael Bolton complains that the singer Michael Bolton has ruined the name "Michael Bolton." Michael's friend Samir suggests that Michael should go by "Mike" instead. Michael responds that the singer, not he, should have to change his name, since the singer is the "one who sucks."

Michael's comment captures an important idea, though it's a farcical case. The singer Michael Bolton is responsible for the "injustice" of making awful music and ruining the name *Michael Bolton*. Therefore, the singer, not the office worker, should have to bear the costs of fixing the problem. Of course, singer Michael Bolton's music is not really an injustice—much as I hate to admit it, having suffered through many car rides with my mom playing him on the radio. Yet the basic idea seems correct.

The burdens of injustice should as much as possible fall on the perpetrators, not on the victims or bystanders. People have a right not to be subject to injustice. But if so, if it's something they are by right owed, then it's not something that they should generally have to *pay* for.

That last claim may sound too strong. After all, people have a right to life and to have their property protected, but most think it's reasonable that people should have to pay some taxes to support the legal structure that protects those rights, or should pay to install door locks and burglar alarms. Still, in some sense, that's too bad. We put up with that because it's the best we think we can do given how unjust we expect others to be. In a perfectly just world, people would simply respect one another's rights, and we wouldn't have to pay to enforce these rights. In a slightly less than perfectly just world, we would find a way to make the rights violators bear the full costs of their rights violations and would require rights violators to make their victims whole. But since we don't know how to do that, we settle for making those who are innocent pay to protect their own rights.

That said, notice that many of our practices and commonsense moral intuitions support the idea that the costs of wrongdoing should fall as much as possible on the wrongdoer rather than the innocent. We allow people who are wrongfully harmed to sue for and recover damages. You are not required, based on the commonsense theory of self-defense and the defense of others, to treat the perpetrator's life as on par with the victim's. After all, it's not like when we see a man trying to murder a woman, we say, "Well, a life's a life, so I guess we have to flip a coin to see whether we should kill the murderer (if necessary) or let him kill the woman. Either way, we save exactly one life." Rather, during the moral emergency, we regard the perpetrator as morally liable to be harmed or even killed. We don't treat the perpetrator's life as equally worthy of protection as the victim's because the perpetrator is responsible for the problem.

ANOTHER MOTIVATING IDEA: THE COST OF RESISTANCE MATTERS

Imagine you have a magic wand. Waving that wand once would magically prevent all future injustice. You've got nothing better to do right now. But you decide not to bother because you aren't yourself harming anyone, and it's not your job to stop injustice, you say.

Now imagine a different case. You have a much lousier magic wand. It weighs two hundred pounds, is covered in angry fire ants, and takes seventy-five hours of constant waving to activate. If you wave it, it will stop some teenager from stealing a pack of cigarettes once. Must you wave it?

Your considered judgment here might be different from mine. Still, my guess is that you think it is obligatory to wave the magic wand in the first case and not the second. In the first case, you can do an incredible amount of good—more good than anyone has ever done—with

214 • Chapter 8

insignificant effort. In the second one, you stop an insignificant injustice at great personal expense. So this suggests a general principle: we have some general though imperfect duty to fight injustice on behalf of strangers, but the expected costs and benefits of the fight matter. When the expected costs to you greatly exceed the expected benefits of your attempt to fight injustice, you generally do not have to fight.

A utilitarian would of course say that whether one has a duty to resist is entirely a matter of cost-benefit analysis. If the expected benefits of resistance exceed the expected costs (including one's opportunity cost), then one has a duty to resist, but otherwise one does not.

Still, admitting that the expected costs and benefits of resistance matter does not commit you to saying that cost-benefit analysis is the entire story. One could just say that these considerations matter, but they are not the only things that do. When the expected costs of resistance greatly exceed the expected benefits, this normally means you have no duty to resist. But you could agree to that and still hold that when the expected benefits of resistance *slightly* exceed the expected costs (including the opportunity costs), you do not thereby have a duty to resist.

SPECIAL OBLIGATIONS CAN CHANGE THE CALCULUS

We owe certain obligations to all people. For example, I owe it to everyone to respect their right to free speech. Philosophers often call these general duties, owed to all, "natural duties." (If you don't like the word "natural," then feel free to use a different label, such as general or basic duties, or whatnot.) Other obligations we owe only to specific people in virtue of the relationships we have with them. I owe it to my children, for instance, to ensure that they are fed, educated, clothed, and loved, but I don't have such duties to strangers' children. A lawyer owes it to her client to give her good legal advice; she has no such duty to strangers at large. I owe it to my students at Georgetown to help them write better papers, but I don't owe such advice to students at nearby George Washington University or George Mason University. Philosophers use the term "special obligations" to refer to duties one owes to a specific subset of people in virtue of the special relationship one has to them.

In some instances, if not all, people who have special obligations to others owe it to those other people to protect them from injustice. They might have stronger or more stringent duties to defend *others* than they have to defend themselves. Consider two cases:

1. As Ann sits on the bus, two elderly women direct a racial slur at her.

2. As Ann and her daughter sit on the bus, two elderly women direct a racial slur at them.

It's plausible to conclude that Ann has stronger reasons to speak up in the second case than in the first. In the first situation, you might think that Ann has significant personal prerogative to decide when and where to defend herself. She just wants to ride the bus and might decide it's not worth having a verbal argument. But in the second case, she has to protect her daughter and make it clear to her daughter that she can count on her mother. So you might conclude that she has a duty to speak up, or at least stronger reasons to do so, in the second instance than in the first.

I won't explore this issue further here. For the sake of simplicity, let's confine ourselves to thinking about cases where there are no such special obligations. After all, whether one is obligated to resist on behalf of those with whom one has a special obligation depends on the nature of the special relationship. There are hundreds of special relationships—married couples, parent and child, brother and sister, broker and client, teacher and student, priest and parishioner, doctor and patient, cousin and cousin, and so on—and the details will vary with each of these relationships. A lawyer has a duty to resist on behalf of her clients only in specific ways in specific contexts, while a parent has a more general duty to protect her child from all sorts of threats. Thus, for simplicity's sake, let's just consider cases of self-defense and the defense of others, where the others are strangers to whom one only owes natural duties. Is there a general *duty* to resist or instead just mere *permission* to do so? If there is a duty, is it perfect or imperfect?

THE COMPLICITY ARGUMENT

One might to try arguing that there is a duty to resist because there is a general duty to avoid complicity with injustice or at least a duty to avoid neutrality. Dante famously places morally indifferent human beings as well as the angels who remained neutral during Lucifer's rebellion in the vestibule of hell, where they are forever forced to race after a banner while horseflies and wasps sting them. In Dante's moral calculus, the morally neutral are better than wrongdoers, but they are still condemned. Or consider this famous poem, derived from a number of speeches by Martin Niemöller:

First they came for the Socialists, and I did not speak out—
because I was not a Socialist.

Then they came for the Trade Unionists, and I did not
speak out—
because I was not a Trade Unionist.

Then they came for the Jews, and I did not speak out—
because I was not a Jew.

Then they came for me—and there was no one left to
speak for me.[2]

What Niemöller means to do, of course, is condemn the German intellectuals who remained silent while the Nazis persecuted their victims.

Dante and Niemöller both seem to think that remaining neutral during a moral emergency is itself a blameworthy behavior, if not as bad as actively *helping* produce an injustice. The worry here is that a person who does nothing is, if not at fault for the injustice, at fault for not taking a stand.

It's worth noting that Neimöller, though he at first supported the Nazis, eventually did speak out. For his efforts, he spent seven years in a concentration camp and barely escaped death. As far as we know, he did not save a single socialist, trade unionist, or Jew from persecution. (Perhaps, though, he later inspired others to resist in more successful ways.)

One might be tempted to make an argument as follows:

1. It is wrong to remain neutral in the face of a moral crisis.

2. If one fails to defend others from injustice, one remains morally neutral.

3. Therefore, it is wrong to fail to defend others, and one has a moral duty to defend them.

This popular argument tries to move from the wrongness of neutrality to the claim that one has a duty to resist injustice on behalf of others.

Let's take a closer look at the first premise. What does it mean to remain neutral? We can distinguish here between neutral *attitudes* and *actions*. Consider that I haven't done anything to stop the rapes, civil war, genocide, and displacement occurring in the Sudan over the past fifteen years. (I donate money and time to some causes, but I have done nothing to help Sudan, as far as I remember.) So my actions are neutral: I am neither helping nor hurting the cause there. Still, my attitudes are not neutral; it's not like I don't care.

The problem with the "neutrality is wrong" argument is that we need some justification for the first two premises, and it's not clear what it could be. We want some independent argument for these premises that does not simply beg the question.

To make the first two premises do the work they need to do, we might interpret the term "moral neutrality" to include failing to act against the injustice. But then the argument merely claims that a person acts wrongly by not stopping the injustice *because* it is wrong not to try to stop an injustice. The reasoning simply says, "Moral neutrality, by which I mean to include failing to resist, is wrong, so therefore it's wrong to fail to resist." It begs the question. If, on the other hand, we don't load "failing to resist" into the definition of moral neutrality, then we need some further argument for why this kind of neutrality is wrong.

A better version of this argument holds that one must avoid *complicity* with injustice. A person is complicit with injustice when one encourages, aids, or abets a person who commits an injustice, and when one shares the intention to complete the crime. In general, a person is not complicit simply because she fails to stop a crime.[3] Rather, the person must materially participate in committing the crime. Moreover (at least on the legal definition of complicity), she must *intend* to help cause the crime.

Here's an illustration. Jalapeño Loco was a Mexican restaurant in Mentor, Ohio. In 2008, federal agents raided it. Supposedly, the restaurant's owners had trafficked undocumented immigrants, who were then "forced to staff the restaurant for long hours and little pay to work off smuggling fees and rent."[4] Let's say the charges are correct and the workers were in effect slaves. Now consider two different people:

- *Cyndi frequently eats at Jalapeño Loco. She is unaware that the kitchen staff members are being forced to work.*
- *Tom works for Jalapeño Loco. He knows the kitchen staff members are forced to work. He assists the restaurant by buying handcuffs and yelling at the enslaved workers.*

Both Cyndi and Tom end up "helping" the restaurant to enslave its workers in the sense that they both undertake actions that make it more likely the workers will remain enslaved. But their situation is different. Cyndi lacks a guilty mens rea; she doesn't know what's happening. She does not intend to enslave the workers. It's not even an unintended but foreseeable (to her) outcome of her patronage. On the other hand, Tom actively participates in the crime.

One might argue that failing to stop injustice means one is complicit in injustice. Yet this is an abuse of the concept of complicity. In general, a complicit person *helps* cause the injustice. He does not merely *fail* to stop it. Under the law, at least, the typical person cannot be charged with complicity simply because she knew about an injustice and failed to report it. The law maintains that people are complicit for failing to stop injustices only if they are special people holding special offices. For instance, certain government agents have a legal duty to stop other agents from abusing their power, while school-teachers, doctors, and a few others have a legal duty to report child abuse to the authorities. One is typically complicit for failing to stop injustice only if one has a prior obligation to stop it.

Now one might retort that the laws are mistaken and overly permissive; they do not reflect the moral truth. One might say instead that we all count as complicit whenever we fail to resist or prevent any injustice we know about and could prevent. Even if that were true, though, it means that introducing the concept of complicity here isn't doing any work. It's just begging the question. To see why, consider this argument:

1. Complicity with injustice is wrong.

2. If complicity with injustice is wrong, then failing to resist is wrong.

3. Therefore, failing to resist is wrong.

As written, this argument seems unsound, because the second premise seems false. The common definition of complicity holds that merely failing to resist or stop an injustice you know about is not a form of complicity. But if a philosopher insists that this should be regarded as a form of complicity, then the argument can be rewritten as follows:

1. Complicity—by which I mean to include failing to resist or prevent injustice—is wrong.

2. If complicity with injustice is wrong, then failing to resist is wrong.

3. Therefore, failing to resist is wrong.

Now it's clear that loading up the concept of complicity does not work. The argument just pounds the table and begs the question. The conclusion follows trivially from the premises. We now need an independent argument for the first premise.

These kinds of arguments are false starts because they beg the question, or at least don't provide a compelling independent justification for their conclusions. We need independent reasons to establish that people have a general duty to resist injustice. If we can find some such arguments, then we could conclude that people who fail to resist are wrongfully neutral or complicity. We won't get anywhere, however, by simply loading up the terms "neutral" or "complicit," such that when we say it's wrong to be neutral or complicit, we're just asserting the very thing we're supposed to prove. So with that, let's turn to some independent assertions.

HAY'S KANTIAN ARGUMENT FOR RESISTANCE

In a recent article, Carol Hay argues that citizens have a duty to resist oppression. She bases her argument on Kantian moral theory—a theory that gives pride of place to respecting and promoting individuals' autonomy and rational nature. She contends that oppression has the following harmful features:

1. Oppression can cause self-deception. The subjugation of women, for instance, might cause women to falsely believe they are inferior or incompetent.

2. Oppression can harm the capacity for rational deliberation. For example, if oppression leads to starvation, this may cause brain damage that permanently reduces the agent's ability to think critically or deliberate.

3. Oppression can cause weakness of will. Perhaps, say, if a person internalizes a negative stereotype (e.g., all Irish people are belligerent drunks), then that person will act in accordance with that stereotype ("I'm Irish, so I guess I can't help but drink and fight").[5]

Hay is right that oppression can cause these problems. Thus, her article is helpful in bringing to our attention to some of the hidden or less obvious harms of oppression.

But let's consider some of the other problems with oppression. Government injustice and oppression can cause starvation, death, suffering, war, economic deprivation, and civil or economic rights violations. When government agents act badly, they might exacerbate crime, remove citizens' economic opportunity, or simply cause direct physical and mental harm. They can deprive citizens of freedom or even their lives. Oppression, Hay agrees, already has all these horrific effects. Hay is correct that we can add *another* three horrible effects to the list. Yet on their face, the three new problems that Hay identifies are far less bad than the direct, obvious effects of oppression. Even from a Kantian perspective, violating someone's rights, murdering them, and so on, are all worse forms of oppression than causing akrasia, self-deception, or other second-order psychological effects.

Thus, adding Hay's three items to our list should not convince us that we have a duty to resist, if we didn't already think that there is such a duty. Are these three items the straw that broke the camel's back? That seems implausible.

Kantians frequently have an absolutist view about the value of rational agency. People are supposed to prioritize rational agency above all else. Frankly, though, it's not a plausible view. For instance, suppose a genie came to me and made the following deal: "I will permanently reduce your capacity for rational deliberation by 1 percent. This will not be enough to cause you to do any more wrongful actions than you otherwise would have. But as part of the deal, I will make you 200 percent happier." It seems reasonable to take that deal. Sure, the capacity for rational deliberation matters, but it can't matter that much, can it? Kant may have arguments to the contrary, but in truth, they are bizarre and not worth repeating here.

Suppose we grant that Hay's new items break the camel's back and establish a duty to resist. We can then ask, Does this mean one must resist *every* instance of oppression one witnesses? Hay answers no, as this would make the duty to resist oppression absurdly demanding:

> There are many different forms that resistance to oppression can take. Thinking about the obligation to resist one's oppression in this way—as an obligation that can be fulfilled by more than one kind of action—makes the obligation what Kantians call an *imperfect duty*. The distinguishing characteristic of imperfect duties is that they permit a wider range of acceptable actions in fulfilling them than is the case for perfect duties. This is because (unlike perfect duties) imperfect duties are not, strictly speaking, duties to perform specific *actions*. Rather, imperfect duties are duties to adopt certain *general maxims*,

or principles of action. These maxims can be satisfied by more than one action. Imperfect duties thus allow a latitude of choice that perfect duties do not. To say that the duty to resist one's oppression is imperfect, however, is not to suggest that it is less stringent or less important than other duties. Instead, calling this duty imperfect means there is a strict duty to set the end of resisting one's own oppression, but there can be more than one way to go about pursuing this end. What the imperfect duty to resist one's oppression rules out is the refusal to do anything to resist one's oppression. That is, it rules out acquiescing in one's own oppression.[6]

Hay claims that all her argument establishes is an imperfect duty to resist oppression. This imperfect duty gives the agent wide latitude to decide which actions to undertake to resist oppression, and which actions to refrain from taking to resist oppression.

Thus, in the end, Hay agrees with my thesis here. She says there is a general and imperfect duty to resist oppression, which the agent has wide latitude in determining how to fulfill it. But my question at the beginning of this chapter was, When a civilian is in situations like A–M or A'–M', is the civilian obligated to act in self-defense or the defense of others in that moment? Hay agrees the answer is usually no.

SILVERMINT'S EUDAIMONIST ARGUMENT FOR RESISTANCE

Daniel Silvermint also maintains that there is a duty to resist oppression. While Hay rests her argument for a duty to resist on Kantian concerns, Silvermint tries instead to assert that the duty to resist is a *self-regarding* duty grounded on a concern for one's own well-being. But as we'll see, Silvermint's argument has more or less the same limitations as Hay's.

Self-regarding duties are those that a person owes to himself rather than to others. For example, perhaps I owe it to myself to develop my talents as opposed to letting them go to waste. Or perhaps I owe it to myself to stand up for myself rather than accept others' burdens or tolerate verbal abuse. Perhaps I owe it myself to learn to love again after a devastating betrayal. And so forth.

Sometimes laypeople talk as if morality concerns only what we owe to each other, but most moral theorists throughout history have contended that we also have self-regarding duties.

I'm inclined to think they're right. But the puzzle remains, Which duties, if any, do we owe ourselves? Do we owe it to ourselves to resist oppression, and if so, why? If so, is the duty to resist a perfect or imperfect one?

Silvermint's strategy for defending a duty to resist is the same as Hay's. He makes a list of the putative benefits of resistance and costs of nonresistance, claiming the following:

1. Resistance "asserts one's status as a moral equal."[7]

2. Resistance expresses that one has self-respect.

3. Resistance is an autonomous response to oppression.

4. Compliancy and conformity may lead to material comfort, but they prevent the oppressed agent from flourishing.

5. Resistance can give the agent "confidence in [his] merit as a person."[8]

6. Resistance can boost the agents' self-esteem.

Silvermint makes a good case for each of these items. I won't repeat his defense here, but just grant him for the sake of argument that resistance indeed carries each of these benefits, while compliance with oppression comes with serious costs.

Note that Silvermint does not intend to show that you have a duty to resist every act or severe wrongdoing you encounter. Instead, he means to focus more narrowly on resistance to *oppression*. He says,

> On my view oppression is a social circumstance that systematically and wrongfully burdens a victim's autonomy or overall life prospects. Oppression is thus a kind of effect, often the cumulative effect of diffuse norms, actions, practices, and institutions. And it is the kind of effect that saturates all or nearly all domains of an individual's life, and does so stably over time.... [O]ppression is a defining feature of a victim's normative situation.[9]

For Silvermint, to be oppressed, one has to be subject to *systematic* injustice. Blacks in the United States who are frequently mistreated by the legal system are oppressed. Women in Saudi Arabia are oppressed. But you aren't oppressed just because you were mugged once. Silvermint isn't talking about momentary injustices; he is speaking of systematic burdens.

Silvermint argues that there is a duty to resist oppression, yet he does not intend for that to mean that you have a duty to resist every wrongdoing you encounter. In *Shooter in the Park* (case A from chapters 1 and 2), the shooter tries to murder children, but he does not *oppress*.

Silvermint also intends for the duty to resist to be an imperfect one:

> If a victim resisted every single oppressive norm and practice encountered daily, their unending resistance would

likely crowd out other valuable aims that contribute to well-being. Defying oppression is necessary to lead a self-respecting and self-directing life, but a life that is only about defiance is probably lacking in other ways. For most victims, protecting and promoting their well-being involves striking a balance between resistance and non-resistance. Some victims might wholeheartedly believe that resistance is all that matters for a worthwhile life, but considerations of well-being certainly do not require that victims do nothing with their lives aside from resist, or even that victims regard resistance as their most important, character-defining endeavor.[10]

Silvermint says there is perhaps no precise, general theory of just how the balance must be struck. But he agrees with me that you should not become a conscript in the Army of Justice merely because you are a victim of oppression. He concurs that you have a personal prerogative to lead the life that's good for you. Indeed, his argument is meant to show that you should (in ways largely up to you) resist your oppression precisely because it serves your interests to do so.

Remember, I discuss Hay and Silvermint here because they are two leading political philosophers who have recently maintained that there is a duty to resist oppression. But notice that they do not argue that we have perfect duties to resist any injustice we encounter. They only contend that we have imperfect duties to rectify systematic oppression.

That said, I worry that Silvermint's argument has the same issues as Hay's. Silvermint has pointed out a number of less obvious or hidden benefits that come from resisting oppression, and hidden costs that come from compliance. It's nevertheless puzzling why adding Silvermint's items to our list would be enough to convince us that we have a duty to resist if we didn't already think that. As I said in response to Hay, government injustice and oppression can cause starvation, death, suffering, war, economic deprivation, and civil or economic rights violations. When government agents act badly, they might exacerbate crime, remove citizens' economic opportunity, or simply cause direct physical and mental harm. They can deprive citizens of freedom or even their lives. If these costs are not enough to show that there is an imperfect duty to resist oppression, why would adding Silvermint's six or so benefits and costs be enough to demonstrate that there is a such a duty?

SINGER'S CONSEQUENTIALIST ARGUMENT

Peter Singer famously asserts that we have stringent duties to rescue others from poverty, disease, and death, even at great personal expense.[11] In Singer's writings on this topic, his goals are to show that we as individuals should donate much more of our income to charity than most of us do, and that governments and nongovernmental organizations should engage in more transfers from the developed world to the developing one. To my knowledge, he has not discussed whether we have an obligation to employ defensive actions. His argument for why we ought to give more to charity, however, could easily be modified to be an argument for why we have a duty to resist on our own or others' behalf.

In this section, I'll first outline his reasoning for why we have a duty to rescue the poor though charity. Then I'll explain how we can modify this argument so it can reflect why we have a duty to engage in defensive action. I'll then offer a critique of Singer's argument. My ultimate conclusion will be that Singer has not really shown us that we have stringent duties of rescue.

Singer has a simple, clear, and powerful argument for the conclusion that each of us should give significantly more to charity than we do. The argument comes in a stronger and weaker version.[12]

Singer's Main Argument

1. "Suffering, and death from a lack of food, shelter, and medical care are bad."[13]

2. The Singer principle (strong version): "If it is in our power to prevent something bad from happening, without thereby sacrificing anything of comparable moral importance, we ought, morally, to do it."[14]

3. The empirical claim: It is within our power to prevent suffering and death from a lack of food, shelter, and medical care by donating money to charity.

4. Therefore, we should donate money to charity

This strong version, Singer thinks, implies most first world people should donate nearly all their income—anything more than what they need for basic necessities—to charity. Singer also offers a weaker version of the second premise. This version is less demanding, but still requires a great deal from us.

2'. The Singer principle (weak version): If it is in our power to prevent something bad from happening without sacrificing anything of moral significance, then we ought, morally, to do it.

Singer thinks the stronger version leads to the conclusion that we should donate most of our money to charity. The weaker version doesn't require that we impoverish ourselves to help others, but it does necessitate that we give away much more than most of us do.

This argument can be modified in defense of a duty to engage in defensive action:

1. Suffering and death from government injustice, violence, and abuse are bad.

2. The Singer principle (weak version): If it is in our power to prevent something bad from happening without sacrificing anything of moral significance, then we ought, morally, to do it.

3. The empirical claim: In certain situations, we can prevent suffering and death from government injustice, violence, and abuse by engaging in defensive actions.

4. Therefore, in those situations, we ought to engage in defensive actions.

The weaker version is open-ended: it tells us that we should always do whatever it takes to stop bad things from happening, provided we can do so without sacrificing anything of moral significance. Singer thinks that it's easy to show that this principle requires almost every first world citizen to give significant portions of their income to charity. Consider that the United States places the poverty line for an American living alone at $11,500. A person living in the United States off this meager income, with a cost-of-living adjustment, is still among the richest 15 percent of people alive today—and earns many times the income of the typical person worldwide.[15] Furthermore, it's now easy to find an effective charity: you can just go to GiveWell.org and donate to one of its top-four picks.

When we apply the Singer principle to questions of injustice, it's more difficult to determine what it requires, because the empirical issues are more complicated. One might think it requires us to lobby or vote for social change, such as for police reform or to shut down the National Security Agency's spying. But as individuals, we can do little; individual votes count for almost nothing, and it's nearly impossible for most of us to organize a political group that realistically could reform bad government. In contrast, when I give $1,000 to Evidence Action's Deworm the World Initiative, I can reasonably expect to deworm over eighteen hundred children.[16] The Singer principle seems to say that we have a duty to use defensive action only when we're in the right place at the right time. For most civilians, that arguably will *never* require us to engage in defensive action against government, because most of us will never be in a situation like A'–M'. Yet citizens who work for their governments will have more frequent opportunities to engage in defensive deceit or sabotage.

The second premise of Singer's argument does the heavy lifting. But is there any reason to believe in that premise?

Singer offers the following thought experiment, which many people read as providing intuitive support for the Singer principle:

One Drowning Child

If I am walking past a shallow pond and see a child drowning in it, I ought to wade in and pull the child out. This will mean getting my clothes muddy, but this is insignificant, while the death of the child would presumably be a very bad thing.[17]

Almost everyone agrees that in this instance, they are obligated to help the child; it would be wrong—a violation of duty, and not just *uncharitable*—to walk away. Sure, saving the child might ruin your $100 pair of pants and $200 shoes, but you *must* do so. But, Singer asks, if you agree that you should sacrifice $300 of clothes to save a drowning child, then why not right now give away $300 to save a child dying of starvation?

So one argument in favor of the Singer principle goes as follows:

1. In the drowning child scenario, you are obligated to save the child.

2. The Singer principle is the best explanation for why you are obligated to save the child in the drowning child thought experiment.

3. Therefore, the Singer principle is true.

When people first read what I call "Singer's Main Argument" above, they generally dispute the second premise, the Singer principle. They think it's too demanding. But when they read Singer's drowning child thought experiment, they agree that they *must* save the child. They then wonder, Since they are committed to saving the child, does that mean that they must endorse the Singer principle? Is the Singer principle what explains their intuition that they must save the child? For Singer, the drowning child thought experiment is what does the work.

Now Singer himself would dispute this reading of his argument. Officially, in his article "Famine, Affluence, and Morality," he does not claim that the reason you should endorse the Singer principle is because it explains or generalizes your intuitions in the drowning child scenario. Rather, he says that the drowning child is simply an instance or application of the Singer principle. He uses it to illustrate *how* the principle works; he does not claim that the thought experiment provides intuitive evidence that the principle is true.[18]

But frankly, even if in Singer's view his argument does not officially rely on the intuition behind one drowning child, that intuition *is* doing most of the work. People find Singer persuasive *because* they think they cannot consistently hold that they must save the one drowning child, and are permitted to refrain from donating most of their income to charity. Singer himself recognizes the persuasive power of the drowning child thought experiment. He begins his recent book *The Life You Can Save* by invoking it, and then uses it to try to get readers to endorse the Singer principle.[19]

So we can ask, If people believe that they must save the drowning child, does that actually commit them to the Singer principle? It seems the answer is no. Consider a new version of the drowning child thought experiment:

Many Drowning Children

You're walking alone one day when you come across hundreds of ponds containing millions of drowning children. You can save some of these children, although doing so will cost you $300 per child. The ones you save will for the most part remain saved, though some might fall back in. No matter how many you save, however, there will be more who are about to drown. You can spend your entire waking life pulling children out of pools.

How many kids must you save, or how many hours a day must you spend rescuing children?

The Singer principle doesn't merely say that you must save a few kids. The strong version holds that you must spend every waking moment saving kids, taking breaks only to feed yourself and do other things that enhance your ability to save kids. The weak version maintains that you must spend most of your life saving children, though you are allowed to have something of a private life.

When I ask my students about these cases, their intuitions about what they should do in the drowning child and many drowning children thought experiments are different. In the one drowning child case, they save a kid and then get on with their lives. In the many drowning children case, saving children could simply *become* their lives. They do not conclude that because you must save the child in the drowning child thought experiment, it follows that you must always save another child no matter how many times in a row you've saved children. Instead, most of them think, "At some point, I've saved enough kids, and I'm allowed to get on with my life, including to do trivial things that are of no moral significance."

Now again, Singer does not see himself as making an intuition-based argument. But again, pace Singer, the reason that most people are inclined to accept his conclusion is because they think their intuitions in cases like the one drowning child require them to accept the Singer principle. When we iterate the drowning child scenario over and over (as the many drowning children situation does), however, they don't judge that they must abide by the Singer principle. So the Singer principle does not appear to offer the best explanation of their intuitions. It's thus not clear why we should accept the Singer principle.

Instead, people seem to believe something else—what we might call the Ross principle, after intuitionist philosopher W. D. Ross:[20]

The Rossian Beneficence Principle

You have a general duty to act beneficently. If you are not destitute, you should give some money to effective charities, and the more you make, the more you should give. In some special cases too, when there is an emergency, you should jump in and help people. But you generally have significant leeway in deciding when and where you will help people. You can live your life, and choose when and how you'll help others.

The Rossian beneficence principle captures commonsense moral thinking. We have a general obligation to help. Sometimes—such as when you encounter your first drowning child—we *must* intervene. Yet we cannot generalize from the one drowning child case to conclude that we must always save every drowning child we can. We have significant prerogative to get on with our lives. Similarly, maybe in some special cases, you have a duty to engage in defensive action on behalf of others. If you can rescue some stranger from injustice at low personal cost and risk, and if you haven't already "done enough," you may have a duty to intervene then and there. Otherwise, the duty is general and imperfect.

CONCLUSION

One important question for political philosophers is when, if ever, an ordinary citizen may justifiably use defensive actions, including defensive violence, against a president, congressperson, bureaucrat, soldier, or police officer, or against government property. That is a dangerous question indeed, but political philosophy must not avoid it just because it might have a dangerous answer.

I have argued that the ethics of defensive action against government or its agents is no stricter than the ethics of defensive action against civilians. The government and its agents do not enjoy any kind of special immunity against defensive action. When government agents commit injustice, they are liable to be deceived, sabotaged, injured, or even attacked, in the same way civilians would be.

To initiate an act of violence against a peaceful, innocent person is almost always wrong. The justificatory bar for initiating aggression is high. But the bar for returning violence against violence, especially in self-defense or the defense of others, is much lower. In commonsense moral thinking, we are permitted to use violence to rescue others from wrongful threats. We are permitted to use violence to defend ourselves along with others from wrongful threats.

Over the past eight chapters, I've examined a wide range of arguments that attempted to show that government agents enjoy special immunity against civilians. Other arguments tried to demonstrate that some government agents at least enjoy special immunity against other government agents or would-be government agents. The arguments all failed. Until we get a successful argument to the contrary, we should conclude that government wrongdoers are morally on par with civilian wrongdoers.

Many of us have seen videos showing the police choke Eric Garner to death.[21] Many have seen "Bou Bou's" battered face after police threw a flash grenade in the sleeping toddlers' crib.[22] The *Washington Post* now runs a column dedicated to documenting and explaining police abuse.[23] One of the most popular genres on YouTube are videos of police violence and citizens refusing to comply with police requests. This is a topic of major current interest. And the problem isn't going away.

Violence is an awful tool. It's not exactly a last resort, but it's rarely a first one. I have not argued for anarchism, violent revolution, or even peaceful revolution. I have not defended a theory of social change, or articulated a platform for revising unjust laws or removing systematic patterns of oppressions. These are difficult problems, and it's unclear whether social scientists have made much progress identifying what works and what does not. My goal here has been quite limited: I have merely argued that you may defend yourself and others from particular acts of government injustice in the same way that you may defend yourself and others from particular acts of civilian injustice.

Government agents have a job to do. In their first instance, their job is to project our rights and implement justice, not to trample our rights and thwart justice. When government agents choose to do the latter, they exceed any putative authority that they might have. When government becomes the enemy, we may protect ourselves. Our rights do not disappear because senators voted to ignore them or because a cop is having a bad day.

Some government agents take on dangerous jobs for our benefit. Police officers assume a great deal of risk, though not as much risk as lumberjacks, farmers, fishers, roofers, truck drivers, or construction laborers.[24] Congresspeople, generals, and presidents take on tremendous, stressful jobs with great responsibility. Their decisions are momentous, and they assume high degrees of moral risk. Judges often have difficult decisions to make too.

At the same time, though, we each possess an inviolability—founded on justice—that forbids anyone from violating our rights. Government agents take on risk, but they also take on greater than normal moral responsibility to protect rather than violate our rights. They should dare not do any less, nor should they expect special immunity if they do so.

Notes

CHAPTER 1

1. This case is based loosely on a real case: Jonah Engel Bromwich, "Videos Show Ohio Police Officer Violently Arresting Black Man," *New York Times*, August 17, 2017, accessed December 6, 2017, https://www.nytimes.com/2017/08/17/us/euclid-ohio-police-brutality.html?mcubz=3.

2. Hirschman 1970, 3.

3. See, for example, Beerbohm 2012.

4. See, for example, Rawls 1971, 355–91.

5. Altman and Wellman 2008, 253.

6. Here I paraphrase McMahan 2009, vii.

7. It's possible that Hirschman regarded resistance as a form of voice.

8. See, for example, Beerbohm 2012.

9. For some defenses of radical pacifism, see Kellenberger 1987; Routley 1984; Filice 1992, 493–95.

10. Cf. David Ferguson, "New Mexico Cop Fired for Shooting at Minivan Full of Kids," Raw Story, December 7, 2013, accessed December 6, 2017, http://www.rawstory.com/rs/2013/12/07/new-mexico-cop-fired-for-shooting-at-minivan-full-of-kids/.

11. Cf. "Rodney King," Wikipedia, accessed December 6, 2017, https://en.wikipedia.org/wiki/Rodney_King.

12. Brennan 2006.

13. Compare this to an incident on May 5, 2011, in which Pima County SWAT team members killed Jose Guerana in his home: Radley Balko, "Jose Guerena Killed: Arizona Cops Shoot Former Marine in Botched Pot Raid," *HuffPost*, August 19, 2011, accessed December 6, 2017, http://www.huffingtonpost.com/2011/05/25/jose-guerena-arizona-_n_867020.html. Note that unlike Ann in my hypothetical case, Guerana did not have any drugs in his home.

14. Hollis Daniels III, a student at Texas Tech University, recently killed a police officer and tried to flee custody when he was arrested for marijuana possession. He was eventually caught and confessed to the killing. David Warren, "Police: Student Confessed to Killing Texas

Tech Campus Cop," *Chicago Tribune*, October 10, 2017, accessed December 6, 2017, http://www.chicagotribune.com/news/nationworld/ct-texas-tech-officer-killed-20171009-story.html. I do not know all the facts of his case, but based on what I know as of October 15, 2017, then yes, this appears to be an instance of permissible violence according to the theory I will defend here. Daniels's actions were highly imprudent, since he had little chance of success, but nevertheless, the officer who arrested and processed Daniels acted unjustly, and was by the theory presented here a rightful target of defensive violence. Of course, this claim also depends on the view that people have the right to use marijuana and that the drug war is unjust. I don't defend that view here, though I think it is rather obviously true. See Huemer 2004; Brennan 2012; Flanigan 2017.

15. Brownlee 2013.

16. Charles Cobb Jr. (2014) argues at length that King accepted nonviolence on strategic rather than purely deontological grounds. King thought that whites would react badly to violence, while nonviolence would lead to more support for the cause of black civil rights. Further, King kept weapons in his home and endorsed violent self-defense as a last resort in many cases.

17. See, for example, Bicchieri 2016; North 1990.

18. Kavka 1995, 2. I insert the qualification "more or less" because no government in history has literally stopped all private violence.

19. See, for example, Huemer 2012.

20. See, for example, ibid.; Leeson 2014; Stringham 2015.

21. See Brennan 2012, 54–80.

22. This quotation comes from US representative Barney Frank. Ross Douthat, "Government and Its Rivals," *New York Times*, January 28, 2012, accessed December 7, 2017, http://www.nytimes.com/2012/01/29/opinion/sunday/douthat-government-and-its-rivals.html.

23. I've noticed that it's become common to respond to some of my arguments as follows: "Brennan is some sort of libertarian, and libertarianism is wrong, so therefore his books *Against Democracy*, *The Ethics of Voting*, *Compulsory Voting: For and Against*, *Markets without Limits*, etc., must be wrong." People say that even though the books do not rely on, presuppose, or require libertarianism, had I been, say, an egalitarian, each of these books would have looked exactly the same.

24. Immanuel Kant himself had things to say about the issues in this book. In some cases he'd take my side, and in others he'd oppose me. But that doesn't mean his *theory* implies those conclusions. There's Kant's theory, on the one hand, and what Kant thinks his theory implies, on the other. Kant thinks his theory implies masturbation is mor-

ally wrong, and that bastard infants should be put to death. Yet—and I say this on Kant's behalf despite being a bastard and former teenage boy myself—Kant is probably just misapplying his theory here. Similarly, there's no straightforward argument from Kant's categorical imperative to most of his particular views about political philosophy. It's the intermediate principles that do the work. For an argument that Kant's political philosophy is not heavily dependent on the categorical imperative, see Ripstein 2009.

25. Gödel 2001.

26. Stephanie Gallman, "Ex-Georgia Deputy Sheriff Indicted in Flash-Bang Raid That Maimed Toddler," CNN, July 22, 2015, accessed December 7, 2017, http://www.cnn.com/2015/07/22/us/georgia -indictment-flash-bang-case/index.html.

27. Sandhya Somashekhar and Steven Rich, "Final Tally: People Shot and Killed 986 People in 2015," *Washington Post*, January 6, 2016, accessed December 7, 2017, https://www.washingtonpost.com /national/final-tally-police-shot-and-killed-984-people-in-2015/2016 /01/05/3ec7a404-b3c5-11e5-a76a-0b5145e8679a_story.html?utm _term=.8ea6b7289410; "Fatal Force: 963," *Washington Post*, accessed December 7, 2017, https://www.washingtonpost.com/graphics/nati onal/police-shootings-2016/.

28. Balko 2013.

29. Julia Angwin, Charlie Savage, Jeff Larson, Henrik Moltke, Laura Poitras, and James Risen, "AT&T Helped U.S. Spy on Internet on a Vast Scale," *New York Times*, August 15, 2015, accessed December 7, 2017, https://www.nytimes.com/2015/08/16/us/politics /att-helped-nsa-spy-on-an-array-of-internet-traffic.html?_r=0; Glenn Greenwald, "Obama Killed a 16-Year-Old American in Yemen. Trump Just Killed His 8-Year-Old Sister," *Intercept*, January 30, 2017, accessed December 7 2017, https://theintercept.com/2017/01/30/obama -killed-a-16-year-old-american-in-yemen-trump-just-killed-his-8-year -old-sister/.

30. Thandisizwe Chimurenga, "The Black Panthers Had the Right Idea," *CounterPunch*, December 11, 2014, accessed December 7, 2017, http://www.counterpunch.org/2014/12/11/the-black-panthers -had-the-right-idea/. It appears that there was only one bystander filming the incident: http://www.latimes.com/local/lanow/la-me-ln-chp -punching-video-marlene-pinnock-charges-20151203-story.html.

31. "OC Weekly: Los Angeles County Deputy Shooting of Noel Aguilar in Long Beach," YouTube, December 18, 2015, accessed December 7, 2017, https://www.youtube.com/watch?v=6I-Xg-Ga1a8.

32. "DA Plays Dash Cam Video in Accidental Shooting; No Charges Will Be Filed," Action News Now, accessed December 7, 2017, http://

www.dailymail.co.uk/news/article-3360037/Shocking-moment-cop
-accidentally-shot-husband-neck-climbed-overturned-SUV-wreck
-killed-wife-NOT-charged.html.
33. See Brennan 2017a.
34. Nock 1929, 345.

CHAPTER 2

1. McMahan 2009, 8–9.
2. Hasnas 2014.
3. LaFave 2003, 570. Here, unlawful means more or less "morally wrong" rather than "illegal."
4. This summarizes and paraphrases ibid., 569–74.
5. See, for example, Hurd 2001.
6. LaFave 2003, 569–82.
7. Hurd 2001, 316.
8. Ibid., 326–27.
9. Altman and Wellman 2008, 253.
10. In DC Comics' *Injustice: Gods among Us*, Superman criticizes Batman for Batman's refusal to kill. In the series, the Joker escapes from prison for the umpteenth time and sets off a nuclear device, killing everyone in Metropolis. Superman points out that Batman *knew* that the Joker would eventually escape, as the Joker always does. Superman holds Batman partially responsible for the destruction of Metropolis. Perhaps that is too strong. Still, we might wonder why Batman takes a principled stance against killing Joker, given that Batman *knows* (he does not merely suspect, but justifiably believes with a high degree of certainty) that his refusal to kill the Joker means that the Joker will kill innocent people in the future. Different versions of the Batman story offer different explanations for why Batman refuses to kill. (Note that in some versions, Batman does kill people.) Most of the explanations given are weak. For example, in *Injustice*, Batman seems to think that if he kills people, this will somewhat corrupt his character. But this seems to commit Batman to a kind of vicious character fetishism. Suppose I could save my children from being murdered by killing their would-be killers, but suppose I know that doing so would permanently reduce my virtue by 10 percent. It seems bizarre and vicious for me to refuse to save them as I would be prioritizing my character over their lives. For further evaluation of this issue, see White 2008.
11. McMahan 2009, 168; Nozick 1974; Thomson 1991.
12. This is a slightly modified version of McMahan 2009, 165. Most philosophers conclude that we can kill Bob, but we have to treat

his life as on par with those of the innocent people we save. So we can't kill him to save one person, but can kill him to save a few dozen.

13. Even Kant most likely accepted that lying could be permissible in special circumstances. See, for example, Mahon, 2009; Varden 2010.

14. When one is merely excused in lying, the act is still wrong, but the lying agent's liability or blameworthiness may be reduced. (So, for instance, if I lie under duress because I am being ordered to do so with a gun to my head, the act is wrong, but I am not blameworthy for it.) When an act is justified, rather than merely excused, the act is not wrong at all.

15. See, for example, Varden 2010; Mahon 2009.

16. Notice in this case that the guard is an innocent aggressor.

17. Marina Fang, "Nearly 90 Percent of People Killed in Recent Drone Strikes Were Not the Target," *HuffPost*, January 3, 2017, accessed December 8, 2017, http://www.huffingtonpost.com/entry/civil ian-deaths-drone-strikes_us_561fafe2e4b028dd7ea6c4ff.

CHAPTER 3

1. The names from these examples come from "food babe" and pseudoscience peddler Vani Hari, philosopher Peter Singer, economist Dani Rodrik, and inventor and government subsidy seeker Elon Musk.

2. Estlund 2008, 2. See also Christiano 2012. In earlier political philosophy, the terms were used in sloppy or nonuniform ways. But in the last ten years or so, it has become the convention to use the terms exactly as I define them here. There is also a sociological concept of legitimacy, associated with Max Weber, where sociological legitimacy refers to a government's perceived authority. This concept of legitimacy is irrelevant to the debate here.

3. Michael Huemer (2012) uses "political authority" to refer to both moral powers. He calls the second power *political obligation*.

4. In Hohfeldian terms, legitimacy refers to a privilege or right to coerce, while authority refers to a claim right and perhaps also a power to coerce.

5. See, for example, Simmons 1996, 19–30. Note that Simmons does not use the words authority and legitimacy the way I do, as the definitions I use became standard later in the literature. For a survey showing how untenable most accounts of political obligation are, see Smith 1996. See also Applbaum 2010.

6. Huemer 2012, 19.

7. Green 2003.

8. Dobos 2017.

9. If you want to read that book, see Huemer 2012.

10. If you've read some of my other works, you've seen me use an example like this involving Fender Telecaster. But I buy lots of guitars.

11. Huemer 2012, 32–33. Huemer cites three separate cases in which the Supreme Court or other major federal courts held that the government has no duties to individual citizens, but only to the public at large.

12. Hart 1955, 185.

13. Thanks to Mike Huemer for this formulation.

14. See Brennan 2016a, 47–48; Huemer 2012, 101–36; Schmidtz and Brennan 2010, 213–16, 226, 236.

15. Simmons makes this point in Wellman and Simmons 2005, 95. He says that even the most die-hard proponents of the duty to obey the law will believe that most legal systems that are, on balance, quite just will include some laws that no one has a duty to obey.

16. This section incorporates an argument I've made in many other places, including Brennan 2016a, 140–71; Brennan 2011b.

17. For what it's worth, while I haven't done a scientific poll, I've presented this example to about two thousand people in dozens of talks over the past few years and most agreed the jury lacked authority in these cases.

18. The relationship between a jury and defendant provides grounds for holding that jurists have something like fiduciary duties toward defendants. The analogy to fiduciary duties, however, appears to understate jurists' obligations. When fiduciaries breach their principals' trust, this is normally considered an intentional tort. Principals can sue their fiduciaries for damages. Yet most fiduciary-principal relationships are contractual and voluntary.

19. As Simmons says, "For many citizens there are few acceptable options to remaining in their states and obeying (most) law, and for most persons active resistance to the state is in effect impossible. And for none of us is there any option to living in some state or other, all of which make (at least) the same core demands on us. These facts raise serious doubts about the voluntariness of any widely performed acts that might be alleged to be binding acts of political consent" (Wellman and Simmons 2005, 118).

CHAPTER 4

1. Estlund 2008, 11, 140.

2. Locke 1980, 11–14.

3. See, for example, Alexander 2013.

4. McMahan 2009, 162.

5. For an extended argument that moral theory aims to explain rather than provide a decision procedure, see Brennan 2008.

6. Brink 1986.

7. Andrew Blake, "Obama-Led Drone Strikes Kill Innocents 90% of the Time: Report," *Washington Post*, October 15, 2015, accessed December 11, 2017, http://www.washingtontimes.com/news/2015/oct/15/90-of-people-killed-by-us-drone-strikes-in-afghani/.

8. Milgram 1963. The next few paragraphs are an edited version of my summary (with David Schmidtz) from Schmidtz and Brennan 2010, 213–14.

9. When Milgram asked in 1963 for predictions, Yale undergraduates predicted an obedience rate of 1.2 percent. Forty Yale faculty psychiatrists predicted a rate of 0.125 percent. See Blass 1999, 963.

10. For a review, see Hewstone, Rubin, and Willis 2002.

11. For further empirical confirmation of this point, see Iqbal and Zorn 2008; Jones and Olken 2009; Spragens 1980.

12. Hurd 2001, 308.

13. Thanks to Mike Huemer for this point.

14. Hurd 2001, 311.

15. Ibid., 331.

16. Ibid., 321.

17. Nozick 1974, 30.

18. One might say, plausibly, that different rights have different weights. The right to choose to eat Gouda cheese is less weighty than the right to determine whom to love and marry. So plausibly, the first right yields to less severe threats than the second one. Nevertheless, note that the rights of self-defense and the defense of others are weighty rights—perhaps among the weightiest we have.

CHAPTER 5

1. "Oath of Enlistment," US Army, accessed December 11, 2017, http://www.army.mil/values/oath.html.

2. "Oath of Commissioned Officers," US Army, accessed December 11, 2017, http://www.army.mil/values/officers.html.

3. Darren Samuelsohn, "Al Gore Is Not Giving Up," *Politico*, April 24, 2014, accessed December 11, 2017, http://www.politico.com/magazine/story/2014/04/al-gore-is-not-giving-up-106003_Page5.html#.WUMg_mVvnzI.

4. One might also believe that the doctor should disclose his conflict of interest. Yet a good deal of empirical psychological research finds that disclosing conflicts of interest *harms* patients or at least backfires. See Loewenstein, Sah, and Cain 2012.

5. See Huemer 2017a.

6. Thanks to Mike Huemer for this formulation.

7. "Police Oath," Wikipedia, accessed December 11, 2017, https://en.wikipedia.org/wiki/Police_oath.

8. Admittedly this is a disputable point. Are police officers fiduciaries of their employers or the public at large? Given that officers usually swear to protect the public, and the public (usually) justifiably reposes confidence and reliance on the police, I'm inclined to see police officers as fiduciaries of the public rather than their employers. This explains, I think, why police corruption and abuse are especially heinous.

9. Estlund 2007.

10. Estlund 2008, 28–29, 275–81.

11. Ibid., 216.

12. Ibid., 33.

13. Gaus 2003, 208.

14. Rawls 1996, 137.

15. For a summary of these commitments, see Gaus 2003, 208–18.

16. David Lefkowitz (2009) also interprets Estlund this way.

17. For a summary of these commitments, see Gaus 2003, 208–18.

18. In technical language, I desire de re that Aiden do something wrong, but desire de dicto that he do what's right, and my de dicto desire is stronger than my de re one.

19. For a thorough theory of epistemic authority, see Zagzebski 2012.

20. Singer 1972; Unger 1996.

21. See Hall 2015.

CHAPTER 6

1. Remember, even Kant most likely accepted that lying could be permissible in special circumstances. See, for example, Mahon 2009; Varden 2010.

2. When one is merely excused in lying, the act is still wrong, but the lying agent's liability or blameworthiness may be reduced. (So, for instance, if I lie under duress because I am being ordered to do so with a gun to my head, the act is wrong, but I am not blameworthy for it.) When an act is justified rather than merely excused, however, the act is not wrong at all.

3. In technical terms, the wizards desire de re to hurt people, but more strongly desire de dicto to help people.

4. Chong 2013, 101; Funk 2000; Funk and Garcia-Monet 1997; Miller 1999; Mutz and Mondak 1997; Feddersen, Gailmard, and Sandroni 2009; Brennan and Lomasky 1993, 108–14; Green and Shapiro

1994; Markus 1988; Conover, Feldman, and Knight 1987; Kinder and Kiewiet 1979; Huddy, Jones, and Chard 2001; Rhodebeck 1993; Ponza, Duncan, Corcoran, and Groskind 1988; Sears and Funk 1990; Caplan 2007; Mutz 1992; Mutz 1993; Citrin and Green 1990; Sears, Lau, Tyler, and Allen, 1980; Sears and Lau 1983; Sears, Hensler, and Speer 1979.

5. Converse 1990, 372.
6. Somin 2013, 17–37.
7. Quoted in Converse 1990, 3.
8. Hardin 2009, 60.
9. Somin 2013, 17–21.
10. Ibid., 31.
11. Ibid., 32.
12. See, for example, Althaus 2003, 11.
13. Ibid., 11–12.
14. Caplan 2007; Caplan, Crampton, Grove, and Somin 2013.
15. Gilens 2012, 106–11; Althaus 2003, 129; Caplan 2007.
16. Gilens 2012, 106–11.
17. Huddy, Sears, and Levy 2013, 11.
18. Westen, Blagov, Harenski, Kilts, and Hamann 2006; Westen 2008; Haidt 2012; Kahan, Peters, Cantrell Dawson, and Slovic, 2017; Tversky and Kahneman 1973; Chong 2013.
19. See, for example, Gilens 2012.
20. See, for example, Schwartzman 2011; Habermas 2001; Rawls 1971, 130, 138; Cohen 2009. Those works, among others, argue that democracy requires "sincerity" or "publicity"—that is, that participants (including politicians) offer sincere and full explanations for what they want to do or are in fact doing.
21. Habermas 2001.
22. Estlund 2008, 6, 75–82.
23. Vallier and D'Agostino 2013.
24. Gaus 1996; Gaus and Vallier 2009; Kang 2003.
25. Schwartzman 2011, 381.
26. Mendelberg 2002, 154.
27. For a review of this research, see Brennan 2016a, 54–73.
28. Mutz 2006, 5.
29. For a summary of these commitments, see Gaus 2003, 208–18.
30. For a further exploration of this issue, see Brennan 2016a.

CHAPTER 7

1. That said, natural law theorists would more or less accept the main idea of this chapter. They would agree judges have a duty to uphold justice independently defined, but would then say that the law

in some way reduces to whatever justice requires of it. In their view, an unjust law is not really a law. I disagree, for the reasons specified, but the normative upshot is the same.

2. For a defense of this view, see Finkelman 2008.

3. This paraphrases and generalizes Huemer 2017b.

4. This is a modification of an example and argument from ibid.

5. An extreme legalist might respond instead that "there are indeed decisive reasons for you not to kill the hermit, burn his garden, and so on. But it's not because the hermit has rights. Rather, it's because utilitarianism is true, and utilitarianism prohibits these things on the grounds that the consequences are bad." This is perhaps the most plausible version of extreme legalism. It allows that there can be decisive moral reasons not to hurt someone, even without legal conventions prohibiting such harms. I won't explore this version in depth here. Yet here is a question and issue: Is this perspective really a rejection of the moderate natural rights, or rather just a particular moral theory of where such rights come from? Further, regardless of the answer, it seems that this view would be compatible with the moral parity thesis as opposed to the special immunity thesis. After all, there are decisive utilitarian reasons not to kill the hermit, so presumably those reasons would remain even if the hermit moved to a society that legalized killing him.

6. For a full defense of this intermediary view, in which the right to property is not fully conventional but not fully natural either, see Huemer 2017b.

7. Nozick 1974, 28–34.

8. Ibid., 30.

9. Ibid., 30.

10. For works that all seem committed to something like this view, see Waldron 1998, 322; Waldron 1999; Shapiro 2003, 9; Fraser 2008.

11. González-Ricoy 2012, 50.

12. Pure proceduralism appears to be an instance of the class of moral theories that Mark Timmons (2012) calls "morality by authority." This class includes divine command theory, subjectivism, and cultural relativism. All four views hold that a particular authority figure or group determines the content of morality or justice. The views just disagree on what the authority figure is and how the figure decides what the content of morality is. The divine command theorist says God arbitrarily chooses the content of morality. The subjectivist says you get to decide it via your feelings. The pure proceduralist maintains that we decide it through some specified political procedure.

13. For a version of this argument, see Gaus 2017.

14. See, for example, Landemore 2012.

15. Achen and Bartels 2016; Brennan 2016a.
16. Mueller 2003.
17. For an account of why the common law is likely to be smarter than statute law, see, for example, Hasnas 2004.
18. See, for example, Levin 1992; US Supreme Court justice Louis Brandeis's dissenting opinion in Burnet v. Coronado Oil & Gas Co., 285 US 393 (1932), 405–10.

CHAPTER 8

1. See Brennan 2011a, 43–67.
2. "Martin Niemöller: 'First They Came for the Socialists … ,'" Holocaust Encyclopedia, United States Holocaust Memorial Museum, accessed December 15, 2017, https://www.ushmm.org/wlc/en/article.php?ModuleId=10007392.
3. Certain special individuals, such as government officials, might be considered complicit by omission, but this holds only when they have special duties by virtue of their office to stop crimes. For example, teachers and doctors are required to report signs of child abuse. But in general, omission is not complicity.
4. Robert L. Smith, "Mentor Restaurant Part of Five-State Raid (Jalapeno Loco in Mentor Is Mentioned, Smuggling Illegals)," *Free Republic*, April 17, 2008, accessed December 15, 2017, http://www.freerepublic.com/focus/f-news/2002768/posts.
5. Hay 2011, 24–27.
6. Ibid., 29–30.
7. Silvermint 2013, 418.
8. Ibid., 420.
9. Ibid., 405–6.
10. Ibid., 422.
11. Singer 1972.
12. See ibid. For a more recent version of essentially the same argument, see Singer 2010, chapter 2.
13. Singer 1972, 231.
14. Ibid.
15. Calculations according to "How Rich Am I?" Giving What We Can, accessed December 16, 2017, http://www.givingwhatwecan.org/why-give/how-rich-am-I; Milanovic 2005.
16. Austin Walker and Katherine Williams, "What Is the Cost of Deworming? A 2016 Update," Evidence Action, July 5, 2016, accessed December 16, 2017, https://www.evidenceaction.org/blog-full/what-is-the-cost-of-deworming-a-2016-update.
17. Singer 1972, 231.

18. Indeed, Singer rejects arguments on the basis of intuitions. He thinks such intuitions and judgments are unreliable, while our considered judgments about abstract moral principles are far more likely to be reliable. See Singer 2005, 350–51.

19. Singer 2010, 3.

20. Ross 1930.

21. "Eric Garner Video: Unedited Version," *New York Daily News*, July 12, 2015, YouTube, accessed December 16, 2017, https://www.youtube.com/watch?v=JpGxagKOkv8.

22. Alison Lynn and Matt Gutman, "Family of Toddler Injured by SWAT 'Grenade' Faces $1M in Medical Bills," ABC News, December 18, 2014, accessed December 16, 2017, http://abcnews.go.com/US/family-toddler-injured-swat-grenade-faces-1m-medical/story?id=27671521.

23. John Sullivan, Derek Hawkins, Kate McCormick, Ashley Balcerzak, and Wesley Lowery, "In Fatal Shootings by Police, 1 in 5 Officers' Names Go Undisclosed," *Washington Post*, accessed December 16, 2017, https://www.washingtonpost.com/policeshootings/?utm_term=.78d2a12022ba.

24. Blake Fleetwood, "Police Work Isn't as Dangerous as You May Think," *HuffPost*, January 15, 2015, accessed December 16, 2017, http://www.huffingtonpost.com/blake-fleetwood/how-dangerous-is-police-w_b_6373798.html.

Bibliography

Achen, Christopher, and Larry Bartels. 2016. *Democracy for Realists*. Princeton, NJ: Princeton University Press.

Alexander, Larry. 2013. "Other People's Errors." *Ethical Theory and Moral Practice* 16:1049–59.

Althaus, Scott. 2003. *Collective Preferences in Democratic Politics*. New York: Cambridge University Press.

Altman, Andrew, and Christopher Heath Wellman. 2008. "From Humanitarian Intervention to Assassination: Human Rights and Political Violence." *Ethics* 118:228–57.

Applbaum, Arthur Isak. 2010. "Legitimacy without the Duty to Obey." *Philosophy and Public Affairs* 38:216–39.

Balko, Randy. 2013. *The Rise of the Warrior Cop: The Militarization of America's Police Forces*. New York: Public Affairs.

Beerbohm, Eric. 2012. *In Our Name*. Princeton, NJ: Princeton University Press.

Bicchieri, Cristina. 2016. *Norms in the Wild: How to Diagnose, Measure, and Change Social Norms*. New York: Oxford University Press.

Blass, T. 1999. "The Milgram Paradigm after 35 Years: Some Things We Now Know about Obedience to Authority." *Journal of Social Psychology* 29:955–78.

Brennan, Jason. 2006. "Marijuana." In *Social Issues in America*, edited by James Ciment, 1044–54. Armonk, NY: M. E. Sharpe.

———. 2008. "Beyond the Bottom Line: The Theoretical Goals of Moral Theorizing." *Oxford Journal of Legal Studies* 28:277–96.

———. 2011a. *The Ethics of Voting*. Princeton, NJ: Princeton University Press.

———. 2011b. "The Right to a Competent Electorate." *Philosophical Quarterly* 61:700–724.

———. 2012. *Libertarianism: What Everyone Needs to Know*. New York: Oxford University Press.

———. 2016a. *Against Democracy*. Princeton, NJ: Princeton University Press.

———. 2016b. "When May We Kill Government Agents?: In Defense of Moral Parity." *Social Philosophy and Policy* 32:40–61.

————. 2017a. "Democracy and Freedom." In *The Oxford Handbook of Freedom,* edited by David Schmidtz. New York: Oxford University Press.

————. 2017b. "Murders at the Ballot Box: When Politicians May Lie to Bad Voters." In *Political Ethics,* edited by Emily Crookston, David Killoren, and Jonathan Trerise, 11–29. New York: Routledge Press.

————, and Peter Jaworski. 2015. *Markets without Limits.* New York: Routledge Press.

Brennan, Geoffrey, and Loren Lomasky. 1993. *Democracy and Decision: The Pure Theory of Electoral Preference.* New York: Cambridge University Press.

Brink, David. 1986. "Utilitarian Morality and the Personal Point of View." *Journal of Philosophy* 83:417–38.

Brownlee, Kimberly. 2013. "Civil Disobedience." *Stanford Encyclopedia of Philosophy,* edited by Edward N. Zalta. Accessed December 6, 2017. https://plato.stanford.edu/entries/civil-disobedience/.

Caplan, Bryan. 2007. *The Myth of the Rational Voter: Why Democracies Choose Bad Policies.* Princeton, NJ: Princeton University Press.

————, Eric Crampton, Wayne A. Grove, and Ilya Somin. 2013. "Systematically Biased Beliefs about Political Influence: Evidence from the Perceptions of Political Influence on Policy Outcomes Survey." *PS: Political Science and Politics* 46:760–67.

Chong, Dennis. 2013. "Degrees of Rationality in Politics." In *The Oxford Handbook of Political Psychology,* edited by David O. Sears and Jack S. Levy, 96–129. New York: Oxford University Press.

Christiano, Tom. 2012. "Authority." In *Stanford Encyclopedia of Philosophy,* edited by Edward N. Zalta. Accessed December 8, 2017. https://plato.stanford.edu/entries/authority/.

Citrin, Jack, and Green, Donald. 1990. "The Self-Interest Motive in American Public Opinion." *Research in Micropolitics* 3:1–28.

Cobb, Charles, Jr. 2014. *This Non-Violent Stuff'll Get You Killed: How Guns Made the Civil Rights Movement Possible.* New York: Basic Books.

Cohen, Joshua. 2009. "Deliberation and Democratic Legitimacy." In *Democracy,* edited by David Estlund, 87–106. Malden, MA: Blackwell.

Conover, Pamela, Stanley Feldman, and Kathleen Knight. 1987. "The Personal and Political Underpinnings of Economic Forecasts." *American Journal of Political Science* 31:559–83.

Converse, Phillip. 1990. "Popular Representation and the Distribution of Information." In *Information and Democratic Processes,* edited by John A. Ferejohn and James H. Kuklinski, 369–88. Urbana: University of Illinois Press.

Dobos, Ned. 2017. "Political Obligation." In *Internet Encyclopedia of Philosophy.* Accessed December 8, 2017. http://www.iep.utm.edu /poli-obl/#SH1a.

Estlund, David. 2007. "On Following Orders in an Unjust War." *Journal of Political Philosophy* 15:213–34.

———. 2008. *Democratic Authority.* Princeton, NJ: Princeton University Press.

Feddersen, Timothy, Sean Gailmard, and Alvaro Sandroni. 2009. "A Bias toward Unselfishness in Large Elections: Theory and Experimental Evidence." *American Political Science Review* 103:175–92.

Filice, Carlo. 1992. "Pacifism: A Reply to Narveson." *Journal of Philosophical Research* 17:493–95.

Finkelman, Paul. 2008. "Was *Dred Scott* Correctly Decided?: An 'Expert Report' for the Defendant." *Lewis and Clark Law Review* 12:1219–52.

Flanigan, Jessica. Forthcoming. *Pharmaceutical Freedom.* New York: Oxford University Press.

Fraser, Nancy. 2008. *Scales of Justice.* New York: Cambridge University Press.

Funk, Carolyn. 2000. "The Dual Influence of Self-Interest and Societal Interest in Public Opinion." *Political Research Quarterly* 53: 37–62.

———, and Patricia Garcia-Monet. 1997. "The Relationship between Personal and National Concerns in Public Perceptions of the Economy." *Political Research Quarterly* 50:317–42.

Gaus, Gerald. 1996. *Justificatory Liberalism.* New York: Oxford University Press.

———. 2003. *Contemporary Theories of Liberalism.* Thousand Oaks, CA: Sage.

———. 2017. "The Open Society and Its Friends." *Critique*, January 15. Accessed December 14, 2017. http://www.thecritique.com/arti cles/open-society-and-its-friends/.

———, and Kevin Vallier. 2009. "The Role of Religious Conviction in a Publically Justified Polity." *Philosophy and Social Criticism* 35:51–76.

Gilens, Martin. 2012. *Affluence and Influence.* Princeton, NJ: Princeton University Press.

Gödel, Kurt. 2001. "A Remark about the Relationship between the Theory of General Relativity and Idealistic Philosophy." In *Collected Works: Publications, 1948–1974*, 202–7. Oxford: Oxford University Press.

González-Ricoy, Iñigo. 2012. "Depoliticising the Polls: Voting Abstention and Moral Disagreement." *Politics* 32:46–51.

Green, Donald, and Ian Shapiro. 1994. *Pathologies of Rational Choice Theory.* New Haven, CT: Yale University Press.

Green, Leslie. 2003. "Legal Obligation and Authority." In *Stanford Encyclopedia of Philosophy*, edited by Edward N. Zalta. Accessed December 8, 2017. http://plato.stanford.edu/entries/legal-obligation.

Habermas, Jürgen. 2001. *Moral Consciousness and Communicative Action.* Cambridge, MA: MIT Press.

Haidt, Jonathan. 2012. *The Righteous Mind.* New York: Pantheon.

Hall, Abigail R. 2015. "Drones: Public Interest, Public Choice, and the Expansion of Unmanned Aerial Vehicles." *Peace Economics, Peace Science, and Public Policy* 21:273–300.

Hardin, Russell. 2009. *How Do You Know?: The Economics of Ordinary Knowledge.* Princeton, NJ: Princeton University Press.

Hart, H. L. A. 1955. "Are There Any Natural Rights?" *Philosophical Review* 64:175–91.

Hasnas, John. 2004. "Hayek, the Common Law, and Fluid Drive." *NYU Journal of Law and Liberty* 1:79–110.

———. 2014. "Lobbying and Self-Defense." Special issue, *Georgetown Journal of Law and Public Policy* 12:391–412.

Hay, Carol. 2011. "The Obligation to Resist Oppression." *Journal of Social Philosophy* 42:21–45.

Hewstone, Miles, Mark Rubin, and Hazel Willis. 2002. "Intergroup Bias." *Annual Review of Psychology* 53:575–604.

Hirschman, Albert O. 1970. *Exit, Voice, and Loyalty.* Cambridge, MA: Harvard University Press.

Huddy, Leonie, Jeffrey Jones, and Richard Chard. 2001. "Compassion vs. Self-Interest: Support for Old-Age Programs among the Non-Elderly." *Political Psychology* 22:443–72.

———, David Sears, and Jack S. Levy. 2013. Introduction to *The Oxford Handbook of Political Psychology, 2nd Edition*, edited by Leonie Huddy, Leonie, David Sears, and Jack S. Levy, 1–21. New York: Oxford University Press.

Huemer, Michael. 2004. "America's Unjust Drug War." In *The New Prohibition: Voices of Dissent Challenge the Drug War*, edited by Bill Masters, 133–44. Saint Louis: Accurate Press.

———. 2012. *The Problem of Political Authority.* New York: Palgrave MacMillan.

———. 2017a. "Devil's Advocates: On the Ethics of Unjust Legal Advocacy." In *Ethics in Politics: The Rights and Obligations of Individual Political Agents*, edited by Emily Crookston, David Killoren, and Jonathan Trerise, 285–304. New York: Routledge Press.

———. 2017b. "Is Wealth Redistribution a Natural Rights Violation?" In *The Routledge Handbook of Libertarianism*, edited by Jason Brennan, Bas van der Vossen, and David Schmidtz, 259–71. New York: Routledge Press.

Hurd, Heidi. 2001. "Is It Wrong to Do Right When Others Do Wrong?: A Critique of American Tort Law." *Legal Theory* 7:307–40.

Iqbal, Zaryab, and Christopher Zorn. 2008. "The Political Consequences of Assassination." *Journal of Conflict Resolution* 52:385–400.

Jones, Benjamin, and Benjamin Olken. 2009. "Hit or Miss: The Effect of Assassination on Institutions and War." *American Economic Journal: Macroeconomics* 1:55–87.

Kahan, Dan, Ellen Peters, Erica Cantrell Dawson, and Paul Slovic. 2017. "Motivated Numeracy and Enlightened Self-Government." *Behavioral Public Policy* 1:54–86.

Kang, John. 2003. "The Case for Insincerity." *Studies in Law, Politics, and Society* 29:143–64.

Kavka, Gregory. 1995. "Why Even Morally Perfect People Would Need Government." *Social Philosophy and Policy* 12:1–18

Kellenberger, J. 1987. "A Defense of Pacifism." *Faith and Philosophy* 4:129–48.

Kinder, Donald, and Roderick Kiewiet. 1979. "Economic Discontent and Political Behavior: The Role of Personal Grievances and Collective Economic Judgments in Congressional Voting." *American Journal of Political Science* 23:495–527.

LaFave, Wayne. 2003. *Criminal Law*. 4th ed. Washington, DC: Thomson-West.

Landemore, Hélène. 2012. *Democratic Reason*. Princeton, NJ: Princeton University Press.

Leeson, Peter. 2014. *Anarchy Unbound: Why Self-Governance Works Better than You Think*. New York: Cambridge University Press.

Lefkowitz, David. 2009. "Is There Ever a Duty to Obey Orders in an Unjust War?" University of North Carolina at Greensboro, unpublished manuscript. Accessed December 12, 2017. http://isme.tamu.edu/ISME09/Lefkowitz09.html#_edn9.

Levin, Joel. 1992. *How Judges Reason*. New York: Peter Lang.

Locke, John. 1980. *Second Treatise of Government*. Indianapolis: Hackett 1980.

Loewenstein, George, Sunita Sah, and Daylian Cain. 2012. "The Unintended Consequences of Conflict of Interest Disclosure." *Journal of the American Medical Association* 307:669–70.

Mahon, James Edwin. 2009. "The Truth about Kant on Lies." In *The Philosophy of Deception*, edited by Clancy Martin, 201–4. New York: Oxford University Press.

Markus, Gregory. 1988. "The Impact of Personal and National Economic Conditions on the Presidential Vote: A Pooled Cross-Sectional Analysis." *American Journal of Political Science* 32:137–54.

McMahan, Jeff. 2009. *Killing in War*. Oxford: Oxford University Press.

Milanovic, Branko. 2005. *Worlds Apart: Measuring International and Global Inequality*. Princeton, NJ: Princeton University Press.

Milgram, Stanley. 1963. "A Behavioral Study of Obedience." *Journal of Abnormal and Social Psychology* 67:371–78.

Miller, Dale. 1999. "The Norm of Self-Interest." *American Psychologist* 54:1053–60.

Mueller, Dennis. 2003. *Public Choice III*. New York: Cambridge University Press.

Mutz, Diana. 1992. "Mass Media and the Depoliticization of Personal Experience." *American Journal of Political Science* 36:483–508.

———. 1993. "Direct and Indirect Routes to Politicizing Personal Experience: Does Knowledge Make a Difference?" *Public Opinion Quarterly* 57:483–502.

———. 2006. *Hearing the Other Side*. New York: Cambridge University Press.

———, and Jeffrey Mondak. 1997. "Dimensions of Sociotropic Behavior: Group-Based Judgments of Fairness and Well-Being." *American Journal of Political Science* 41:284–308.

Nock, Alfred Jay. 1939. "The Criminality of the State." *American Mercury* (March): 344–50.

North, Douglas. 1990. *Institutions, Institutional Change, and Economic Performance*. New York: Cambridge University Press.

Nozick, Robert. 1974. *Anarchy, State, and Utopia*. New York: Basic Books.

Ponza, Michael, Greg Duncan, Mary Corcoran, and Fred Groskind. 1988. "The Guns of Autumn? Age Differences in Support for Income Transfers to the Young and Old." *Public Opinion Quarterly* 52:441–66.

Rawls, John. 1971. *A Theory of Justice*. Cambridge, MA: Harvard University Press.

———. 1996. *Political Liberalism*. New York: Columbia University Press.

Rhodebeck, Laurie. 1993. "The Politics of Greed? Political Preferences among the Elderly." *Journal of Politics* 55:342–64.

Ripstein, Arthur. 2009. *Force and Freedom: Kant's Legal and Political Philosophy*. Cambridge, MA: Harvard University Press.

Ross, W. D. 1930. *The Right and the Good*. New York: Oxford University Press.

Routley, Richard. 1984. "On the Alleged Inconsistency, Moral Insensitivity, and Fanaticism of Pacifism." *Inquiry* 27:117–36.

Schmidtz, David, and Jason Brennan. 2010. *A Brief History of Liberty*. Oxford: Wiley-Blackwell Press.

Schwartzman, Micah. 2011. "The Sincerity of Public Reason." *Journal of Political Philosophy* 19:375–98.

Sears, David O., and Carolyn L. Funk. 1990. "Self-Interest in Americans' Political Opinions." In *Beyond Self-Interest*, edited by Jane Mansbridge, 147–70. Chicago: University of Chicago Press.

———, Carl Hensler, and Leslie Speer. 1979. "Whites' Opposition to 'Busing': Self-Interest or Symbolic Politics?" *American Political Science Review* 73:369–84.

———, and Richard Lau. 1983. "Inducing Apparently Self-Interested Political Preferences." *American Journal of Political Science* 27: 223–52.

———, Richard Lau, Tom Tyler, and Harris Allen. 1980. "Self-Interest vs. Symbolic Politics in Policy Attitudes and Presidential Voting." *American Political Science Review* 74:670–84.

Shapiro, Ian. 2003. *The State of Democratic Theory*. Princeton, NJ: Princeton University Press.

Silvermint, Daniel. 2013. "Resistance and Well-Being." *Journal of Political Philosophy* 21:405–25.

Simmons, A. John. 1996. "Philosophical Anarchism." In *For and against the State: New Philosophical Readings*, edited by John T. Sanders and A. John Simmons, 19–30. Boulder, CO: Rowman and Littlefield.

Singer, Peter. 1972. "Famine, Affluence, and Morality." *Philosophy and Public Affairs* 1:229–43.

———. 2005. "Ethics and Intuitions." *Journal of Ethics* 9:331–52.

———. 2010. *The Life You Can Save*. New York: Random House.

Smith, M. B. E. 1996. "The Duty to Obey the Law." In *Companion to the Philosophy of Law and Legal Theory*, edited by Dennis Patterson, 465–74. Oxford: Blackwell.

Somin, Ilya. 2013. *Democracy and Political Ignorance*. Stanford, CA: Stanford University Press.

Spragens, William. 1980. "Political Impact of Presidential Assassinations and Attempted Assassination." *Presidential Studies Quarterly* 10:336–47.

Stringham, Edward. 2015. *Private Governance*. New York: Oxford University Press.

Thomson, Judith Jarvis. 1991. "Self-Defense." *Philosophy and Public Affairs* 20:283–310.

Timmons, Mark. 2012. *Moral Theory: An Introduction*. Boulder, CO: Rowman and Littlefield.

Tversky, Andrew, and Daniel Kahneman. 1973. "Availability: A Heuristic for Judging Frequency and Probability." *Cognitive Psychology* 5:207–33.

Unger, Peter. 1996. *Living High while Letting Die*. New York: Oxford University Press.

Vallier, Kevin, and Fred D'Agostino. 2013. "Public Justification." *Stanford Encyclopedia of Philosophy*, edited by Edward N. Zalta. Accessed December 20, 2017, http://plato.stanford.edu/entries/justification-public/.

Varden, Helga. 2010. "Kant and Lying to the Murderer at the Door … One More Time: Kant's Legal Philosophy and Lies to Murderers and Nazis." *Journal of Social Philosophy* 41:403–21.

Waldron, Jeremy. 1998. "Participation: The Right of Rights." *Proceedings of the Aristotelian Society* 98:307–37.

———. 1999. *Law and Disagreement*. New York: Oxford University Press.

Wellman, Christopher Heath, and A. John Simmons. 2005. *Is There a Duty to Obey the Law: For and Against*. New York: Cambridge University Press/

Westen, Drew. 2008. *The Political Brain*. New York: Perseus Books.

Westen, Drew, Pavel S. Blagov, Keith Harenski, Clint Kilts, and Stephan Hamann. 2006. "The Neural Basis of Motivated Reasoning: An FMRI Study of Emotional Constraints on Political Judgment during the U.S. Presidential Election of 2004." *Journal of Cognitive Neuroscience* 18:1947–58.

White, Mark D. 2008. "Why Doesn't Batman Kill the Joker?" In *Batman and Philosophy*, edited by William Irwin, 5–16. Boston: Wiley-Blackwell.

Zagzebski, Linda Trinkaus. 2012. *Epistemic Authority: A Theory of Trust, Authority, and Autonomy in Belief*. New York: Oxford University Press.

Index